Editor
Stephanie Buehler, M.P.W., M.A.

Editorial Project Manager
Ina Massler Levin

Editor in Chief
Sharon Coan, M.S. Ed.

Illustrator
Ken Tunell

Cover Artist
Denise Bauer

Art Coordinator
Cheri Macoubrie Wilson

Associate Designer
Denise Bauer

Imaging
James Edward Grace

Product Manager
Phil Garcia

Publishers
Rachelle Cracchiolo, M.S. Ed.
Mary Dupuy Smith, M.S. Ed.

Social Studies Games

CHALLENGING

Author

Joyce Gallagher, M.A.

Teacher Created Materials, Inc.
6421 Industry Way
Westminster, CA 92683
www.teachercreated.com
©1999 Teacher Created Materials, Inc.
Reprinted, 2000
ISBN-1-57690-313-3
Made in U.S.A.

Table of Contents

Introduction

Getting students to maintain interest in Social Studies at the middle and junior high school levels can be challenging. *Social Studies Games* is an ideal resource for providing these students with an exciting format for learning and reviewing social studies topics.

Social Studies Games contains 28 card games related to such topics as geography, history, exploration, and government. Many students who think of board games as being for young children will warm up to a good card game.

This book has taken all the work out of making card games for the classroom. All the research has been done and many relevant subject areas are covered. All that's needed is for the teacher to print the pages on card stock, cut them apart, and laminate them so that they will last for years. Enjoy!

How to Use This Book

The games in this book are just about ready to go; only a little time and preparation are required.

Preparing Question Cards

Use a copy machine to copy the cards onto any color of card stock for most games. Some games do require that more than one color of card stock to be used. This is clearly indicated in the "Construction" section and noted at the top of the appropriate pages.

Once the pages containing the cards are copied onto card stock, you may wish to decorate the back of the cards with a sticker such as a small flag or other symbol. Whether you decorate the cards or leave them blank, laminate the sheets and cut the cards apart.

Game Rules and Answer Keys

All of the games have a "rules box." Some of the games are self-checking as the answers are printed right on the card; most have an answer key.

Copy the pages containing the rules box and answer keys onto regular paper, trim, and mount on card stock of the same color that was used for the game cards. Laminate these as well.

Laminating

Laminating can be done with a machine or by hand with clear shelf liner. You may also wish to check with your closest educational supply shop for laminating materials. In order to save laminating film and cutting time, copy the pages first, then trim away the excess edges of each page. Laminate the block of uncut cards, then cut the cards apart.

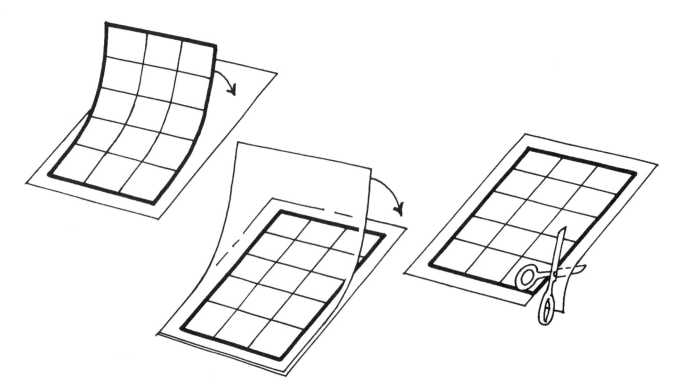

Game Storage

These games take up very little storage space. Whatever storage container you use should be large enough to hold the cards, rules, and answer key together. Here are some storage ideas.

1. Plastic bags with a zipper

This is perhaps the easiest way to store the card games. Simply put the pieces into the bag and use a permanent marker to label it. Keep all the games in a decorated cardboard box.

2. Small, sturdy boxes

Use a small box such as a stationary box, gift box, etc., that is large enough to hold the cards, rules, and answer key. You can decorate the boxes and label each on the outside with the game it contains.

3. Large clasp envelopes

These envelopes are available in manila or brightly colored paper. The envelope can be decorated with a magazine photo that relates to the game topic. Write the title of the game clearly on the back of the envelope. Leave the flap open to laminate the envelope, then use a razor or craft knife to cut the envelope open again. Store the envelopes in a box which will hold them upright so that students can read the title.

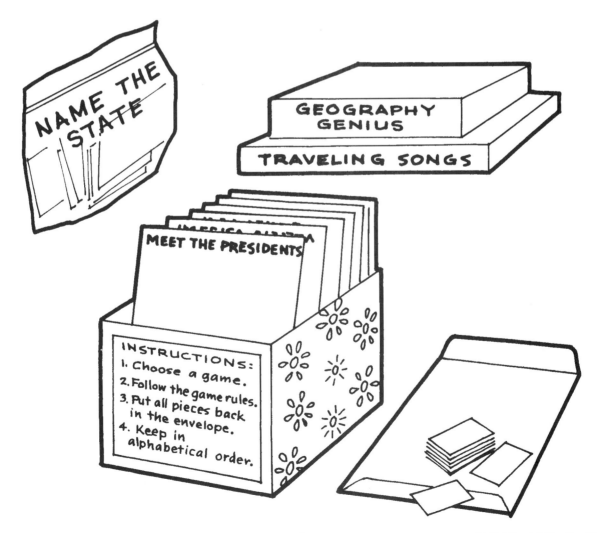

Modifying the Games

The games can be changed in several ways to suit the needs of your classroom.

Add Game Cards

Blank cards in the sizes used throughout this book have been provided on pages 287. Add game cards to the game as follows:

- Choose the appropriate page and make several copies.
- Type additional questions onto the blank cards.
- Copy the prepared questions onto card stock.
- Trim, laminate, and cut the cards apart.
- Adjust the answer key to include answers to the new questions.

Make a New Game

Try using the rules of a game with questions you have created for your own unit of study as follows:

- Make a new game by first making several copies of the appropriate page of blank cards.
- Type questions onto the blank cards.
- Copy the prepared questions onto card stock.
- Trim, laminate, and cut the cards apart.
- Create an answer key for the game.
- Copy, trim, and mount the answer key on card stock, then laminate.
- Print the game title onto a strip of paper and tape it over the prepared rules.
- Copy the new rules onto card stock.
- Trim and mount the rules onto card stock, then laminate.

Using the Games

Most games work best when students are put into groups of three or four. Small groups allow each student more turns at answering questions, giving them less time to become restless while waiting for their turn.

Some games have enough cards to divide the decks into sets so that each group of students has different cards. You may wish to color code these sets of cards in order to keep them sorted into different decks for the same game. For example, if there are 120 cards in a game, you could copy 30 cards onto four different colors of card stock. Also, students can trade cards with another group when they are done with a deck and continue their play.

Students will need instructions on how the games will be used in your classroom. Will the students be able to get out the games if they have finished their assigned work? Will there be a specific game time when students will all play games at the same time? Where and how will the games be stored?

The following rules will help you and the students take care of and use the games.

- Put all the pieces back into their storage container at the end of the game.

- Return games to the proper location in the classroom.

- Keep games in alphabetical order.

- Take care of the cards and/or board games as if they were your own. Games should be played quietly; do not disturb others in the room.

Making Board Games

If you think your students would enjoy board games, any set of cards can be turned into one. To create a board game, do the following:

- Choose a sheet of poster board in any color.

- Use stickers to create a "track" for players to move around. Find stickers that relate to the topic, or use brightly colored adhesive dots. Connect the stickers or dots with a black marker. At the end of the game track, glue a magazine photograph or other picture appropriate to the game theme, e.g., a state capitol building for a game about state capitals.

- Label the board game with the name of the game.

- Provide dice or spinner and playing pieces.

- Adjust the rules so that they fit the board game. For example, instead of keeping a card, the player gets to spin again and move a certain number of spaces.

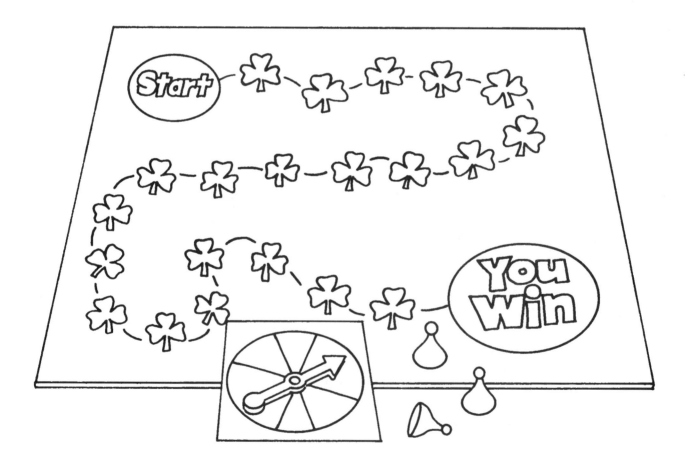

Capital Scramble

This game has 50 cards, each with a scrambled name of a state capital. Players must unscramble the name of the capital city and then identify the state in which the city is located.

Purpose: to reinforce learning about state capitals

Materials Needed:

- card stock of any color to print game cards and to mount rules and answer key
- laminating materials

Construction:

1. Copy game card pages onto colored card stock. Laminate pages, then cut cards apart.
2. Trim rules box and answer key box. Mount them on the same color card stock as used for the game cards and laminate them.

Rules for "Capital Scramble"

This game is for two to three players and one scorekeeper. Paper and pencil are needed for keeping score. Players sit so they may all see each card. Scorekeeper sits opposite the players.

1. Scorekeeper shuffles the cards and places them face down in front of him or her.
2. Scorekeeper turns first card up and places it in front of players.
3. If a player knows the capital city, the player quietly places a hand over the card and says its name.
4. Scorekeeper checks answer key.
5. Scorekeeper scores as follows:

    Correct answer: Win 2 points. Card goes into discard pile.

    Incorrect answer: Lose 2 points. Card goes back into card pile.

6. If a player gives the correct capital, player may try to name the state where the capital is found.

    Correct answer: Win 2 points.

    Incorrect answer: Lose 2 points.

7. When all cards are used or when game time is over, the player with the most points is the winner.

---

1. TUGASAU	2. RENTTON
3. DARTFORH	4. BRUSHGIRRA
5. OHEXPIN	6. MALES
7. CONNILL	8. FREEJOFNS TYIC
9. JONKACS	10. NAPOSILAN

11.	12.
SEEALLHAATS	LOOKHAAM YICT
13.	14.
NOBAT GOURE	LETILT CORK
15.	16.
BARKMISC	LOLOHUNU
17.	18.
FORKTRANF	FLIPEDRINGS
19.	20.
SED MINOSE	TALS KALE TYCI

21. 🏛️

RENTASACMO

22. 🏛️

DIANAINOSLIP

23. 🏛️

PEAKTO

24. 🏛️

VENDER

25. 🏛️

AULMICOB

26. 🏛️

AUJNEU

27. 🏛️

NOSCAR ICTY

28. 🏛️

SEBOI

29. 🏛️

LEANHE

30. 🏛️

YEENCHEN

31. ANSAT EF	32. USTAIN
33. RIPREE	34. NOIMSAD
35. SIGNALN	36. BUSLOCUM
37. SHINVALLE	38. GOTMYERMON
39. ROVED	40. LATTNAA

41. NBOOTS	**42.** TS LAPU
43. CORNDOC	**44.** BAANLY
45. CHIRDMON	**46.** GALEHIR
47. PROVEDNICE	**48.** HARLESTONC
49. NOPEELTRIM	**50.** MOLYAPI

Answer Key for "Capital Scramble"

1. Augusta, Maine
2. Trenton, New Jersey
3. Hartford, Connecticut
4. Harrisburg, Pennsylvania
5. Phoenix, Arizona
6. Salem, Oregon
7. Lincoln, Nebraska
8. Jefferson City, Missouri
9. Jackson, Mississippi
10. Annapolis, Maryland
11. Tallahassee, Florida
12. Oklahoma City, Oklahoma
13. Baton Rouge, Louisiana
14. Little Rock, Arkansas
15. Bismarck, North Dakota
16. Honolulu, Hawaii
17. Frankfort, Kentucky
18. Springfield, Illinois
19. Des Moines, Iowa
20. Salt Lake City, Utah
21. Sacramento, California
22. Indianapolis, Indiana
23. Topeka, Kansas
24. Denver, Colorado
25. Columbia, South Carolina

26. Juneau, Alaska
27. Carson City, Nevada
28. Boise, Idaho
29. Helena, Montana
30. Cheyenne, Wyoming
31. Santa Fe, New Mexico
32. Austin, Texas
33. Pierre, South Dakota
34. Madison, Wisconsin
35. Lansing, Michigan
36. Columbus, Ohio
37. Nashville, Tennessee
38. Montgomery, Alabama
39. Dover, Delaware
40. Atlanta, Georgia
41. Boston, Massachusetts
42. St. Paul, Minnesota
43. Concord, New Hampshire
44. Albany, New York
45. Richmond, Virginia
46. Raleigh, North Carolina
47. Providence, Rhode Island
48. Charleston, West Virginia
49. Montpelier, Vermont
50. Olympia, Washington

Special Places in America

Each card in this game names a place that is either of historical significance or an interesting tourist site in the United States. Players must tell the location of the place named; the game card tells if the location named must be a city, a state, or both a city and its state.

Purpose: to practice and reinforce learning about U.S. sites that have special significance

Materials Needed:

- card stock of any color to print game cards and to mount rules and answer key

- laminating materials

Construction:

1. Copy game cards onto colored card stock. Laminate pages, then cut cards apart.

2. Trim rules box and answer key box. Mount them on the same color of card stock as used for the game cards and laminate them.

Rules for "Special Places in America"

This game is for two to three players and one scorekeeper. Paper and pencil are needed for keeping score. Players sit so that they all may see each card. Scorekeeper sits opposite the players and holds the answer key.

1. Scorekeeper shuffles the cards and places them face down in front of him or her.

2. Scorekeeper turns first card up and places it in front of the players.

3. If a player knows the location of the place named on the card, that player quietly places a hand on the card and says its name. The card tells if players must name a city, a state, or both a city and its state.

4. Scorekeeper checks the answer key and scores as follows:
   Correct answer: Win 2 points. Card goes to discard pile.
   Incorrect answer: Lose 2 points. Card goes back in card pile.

5. When all cards are used or when game time is over, the player with the most points is the winner.

---

1. **CARLSBAD CAVERNS** (state)	**2.** **CRATER LAKE** (state)	**3.** **THE EVERGLADES** (state)
4. **GRAND CANYON** (state)	**5.** **GREAT SMOKY MOUNTAINS** (2 states)	**6.** **HOT SPRINGS NATIONAL PARK** (state)
7. **MAMMOTH CAVE** (state)	**8.** **PETRIFIED FOREST** (state)	**9.** **REDWOOD NATIONAL PARK** (state)
10. **ROCKY MOUNTAIN NATIONAL PARK** (state)	**11.** **YELLOWSTONE NATIONAL PARK** (3 states)	**12.** **YOSEMITE NATIONAL PARK** (state)
13. **MOUNT RUSHMORE** (state)	**14.** **APPOMATTOX COURT HOUSE** (state)	**15.** **MINUTEMAN STATUE** (state)

16.	17.	18.
THE ALAMO (city and state)	**DEATH VALLEY** (2 states)	**DEVIL'S TOWER** (state)
19.	20.	21.
FORT McHENRY (state)	**BADLANDS** (2 states)	**FORT SUMTER** (state)
22.	23.	24.
GEORGE WASHINGTON CARVER NATIONAL MONUMENT (state)	**JOSHUA TREE NATIONAL MONUMENT** (state)	**NATURAL BRIDGES NATIONAL MONUMENT** (state)
25.	26.	27.
ORGAN PIPE CACTUS NATIONAL MONUMENT (state)	**RAINBOW BRIDGE** (state)	**STATUE OF LIBERTY** (city and state)
28.	29.	30.
WHITE SANDS NATIONAL MONUMENT (state)	**GETTYSBURG BATTLEFIELD** (state)	**VICKSBURG NATIONAL MILITARY PARK** (state)

31. ABRAHAM LINCOLN'S BIRTHPLACE (state)	32. FORD'S THEATER (city)	33. THOMAS JEFFERSON NATIONAL MEMORIAL (city)
34. ARLINGTON NATIONAL CEMETERY (state)	35. LINCOLN NATIONAL MEMORIAL (city)	36. WASHINGTON NATIONAL MONUMENT (city)
37. SMITHSONIAN INSTITUTION (city)	38. THE WHITE HOUSE (city)	39. U.S. CAPITOL BUILDING (city)
40. GOLDEN GATE BRIDGE (city and state)	41. NIAGARA FALLS (state)	42. WORLD TRADE CENTER (city and state)
43. EMPIRE STATE BUILDING (city and state)	44. LIBRARY OF CONGRESS (city)	45. SPACE AND ROCKET CENTER (city and state)

46. **PAINTED FOREST** (state)	**47.** **PIKE'S PEAK** (state)	**48.** **KENNEDY SPACE CENTER** (state)
49. **PEARL HARBOR** (state)	**50.** **LINCOLN'S TOMB** (city and state)	**51.** **FORT KNOX** (state)
52. **U.S. NAVAL ACADEMY** (state)	**53.** **MARK TWAIN'S BOYHOOD HOME** (city and state)	**54.** **GREAT SALT LAKE** (state)
55. **LIBERTY BELL** (city and state)	**56.** **WEST POINT MILITARY ACADEMY** (state)	**57.** **WRIGHT BROTHERS NATIONAL MEMORIAL** (state)
58. **BASEBALL HALL OF FAME** (city and state)	**59.** **FOOTBALL HALL OF FAME** (city and state)	**60.** **SUPREME COURT BUILDING** (city)

Answer Key for
"Special Places In America"

1. New Mexico
2. Oregon
3. Florida
4. Arizona
5. North Carolina and Tennessee
6. Arkansas
7. Kentucky
8. Arizona
9. California
10. Colorado
11. Wyoming, Montana, and Idaho
12. California
13. South Dakota
14. Virginia
15. Massachusetts
16. San Antonio, Texas
17. California and Nevada
18. Wyoming
19. Maryland
20. South Dakota and North Dakota
21. South Carolina
22. Missouri
23. California
24. Utah
25. Arizona
26. Utah
27. New York, New York
28. New Mexico
29. Pennsylvania
30. Mississippi

31. Kentucky
32. Washington, D.C.
33. Washington, D.C.
34. Virginia
35. Washington, D.C.
36. Washington, D.C.
37. Washington, D.C.
38. Washington, D.C.
39. Washington, D.C.
40. San Francisco, California
41. New York
42. New York, New York
43. New York, New York
44. Washington, D.C.
45. Huntsville, Alabama
46. Arizona
47. Colorado
48. Florida
49. Hawaii
50. Springfield, Illinois
51. Kentucky
52. Maryland
53. Hannibal, Missouri
54. Utah
55. Philadelphia, Pennsylvania
56. New York
57. North Carolina
58. Cooperstown, New York
59. Canton, Ohio
60. Washington, D.C.

Name the State!

This game has a card for each of the 50 states. Each card gives five clues to help players identify the state. The game can be played in small groups or with the entire class, allowing the first student who stands to give the answer and earn points.

Purpose: to practice and review geographical knowledge about the 50 states

Materials Needed:

- card stock of any color to print game cards and to mount rules box
- laminating materials

Construction:

1. Print game card pages on colored card stock. Laminate pages, then cut cards apart.
2. Trim rules box and mount on card stock of same colors as used for game cards. Laminate.

Rules for "Name the State"

This game is for three players and one scorekeeper. Each player needs scrap paper and pencil for keeping score.

1. Scorekeeper shuffles the cards and places them face down.

2. Scorekeeper turns first card up and reads each clue aloud, pausing after each clue.

3. After hearing any clue, a player may write the name of the state on paper and show it to the scorekeeper.

4. The first player to write the correct state name gets the number of points equal to the number of the clue.

5. Points are recorded and scorekeeper starts with another card.

6. When all cards are used or when game time is over, the player with the most points is the winner.

5- Birthplace of George W. Carver
4- Mobile, a port city on the Gulf of Mexico
3- Space and Rocket Center at Huntsville
2- Abbreviation: AL
1- Capital: Montgomery

(Alabama)

5- Denali National Park
4- U.S. bought it from Russia
3- Nickname: "The Last Frontier"
2- Capital: Juneau
1- Most northern state

(Alaska)

5- More Indians than any other state
4- Painted Desert
3- Petrified Forest
2- Grand Canyon
1- Capital: Phoenix

(Arizona)

5- Nickname: "Land of Opportunity"
4- Hot Springs National Park
3- Home of President Clinton
2- Abbreviation: AR
1- Capital: Little Rock

(Arkansas)

5- More people than any other state
4- Home of President Richard Nixon
3- Death Valley, lowest point in the nation
2- Redwood trees
1- Yosemite National Park

(California)

5- U.S. Air Force Academy
4- Dinosaur National Monument
3- Pike's Peak
2- Rocky Mountain National Park
1- Capital: Denver

(Colorado)

5- Nickname: "Constitution State"
4- Home of Eli Whitney
3- Bordered on the south by the Atlantic Ocean
2- Capital: Hartford
1- Abbreviation: CT

(Connecticut)

5- First state to join the Union
4- Next to the smallest state
3- Largest City: Washington
2- Capital: Dover
1- Abbreviation: DE

(Delaware)

5- Oldest U.S. city is in this state
4- Nickname: "Sunshine State"
3- Cape Kennedy Space Center
2- Everglades National Park
1- Largest city: Miami

(Florida)

5- Okefenokee Swamp
4- Largest state east of the Mississippi
3- Home of President Jimmy Carter
2- Nickname: "Peach State"
1- Capital: Atlanta

(Georgia)

5- First explored by James Cook in 1778 4- Main crops: sugar, pineapple 3- Largest volcano in the world 2- Pearl Harbor 1- Nickname: Aloha State (Hawaii)	5- Bordered by Canada on the north 4- Famous ski resort: Sun Valley 3- Craters of the Moon National Monument 2- Capital: Boise 1- Famous for potatoes (Idaho)
5- Borders Lake Michigan 4- Has one of the nation's three largest cities 3- Capital: Springfield 2- Called "Land of Lincoln" 1- Abbreviation: IL (Illinois)	5- Purdue and Notre Dame Universities 4- Nickname: Hoosier State 3- Southern border: Ohio River 2- Famous car race each year in May 1- Abbreviation: IN (Indiana)
5- Grows more corn than any other U.S. state 4- Birthplace of Herbert Hoover 3- Called the "Hawkeye State" 2- North of Missouri 1- Abbreviation: IA (Iowa)	5- Eisenhower Presidential Library 4- Army forts: Leavenworth & Riley 3- Produces 20% of U.S. wheat 2- Largest city: Wichita 1- Capital: Topeka (Kansas)
5- Mammoth Cave National Park 4- Birthplace of Abraham Lincoln 3- North border is the Ohio River 2- Home of a famous horse race 1- Capital: Frankfort (Kentucky)	5- Looks like a boot 4- Second in U.S. rice production 3- Super Bowl often played in the "Superdome" 2- Nickname: Pelican State 1- Largest city: New Orleans (Louisiana)
5- Acadia National Park 4- Largest New England state 3- Home of poet Henry Wadsworth Longfellow 2- Capital: Augusta 1- Abbreviation: ME (Maine)	5- U.S. Naval Academy 4- "Star Spangled Banner" was written here 3- Donated land to build Washington, D.C. 2- Largest city: Baltimore 1- Abbreviation: MD (Maryland)

5- John F. Kennedy Presidential Library
4- First Thanksgiving held in this state
3- Boston Tea Party
2- Paul Revere's home
1- Capital: Boston

(Massachusetts)

5- First in production of autos
4- Borders 4 of the 5 Great Lakes
3- A peninsula state
2- Capital: Lansing
1- Largest city: Detroit

(Michigan)

5- "Land of 10,000 Lakes"
4- Mesabi Range produces 60% of U.S. iron ore
3- Home of Paul Bunyan
2- Capital: St. Paul
1- Abbreviation: MN

(Minnesota)

5- Second only to Texas in cotton production
4- Nickname: "Magnolia State"
3- Bordered by Mississippi River
2- Capital: Jackson
1- Vicksburg National Military Park

(Mississippi)

5- Where Oregon and Santa Fe Trails began
4- Home of Mark Twain
3- Capital: Jefferson City
2- Home of Harry S. Truman
1- Largest cities: St. Louis and Kansas City

(Missouri)

5- Glacier National Park
4- Largest city: Great Falls
3- Part of Yellowstone National Park
2- Capital: Helena
1- Abbreviation: MT

(Montana)

5- Only state that has a one-house state legislature
4- Oregon Trail crosses this state
3- Chimney Rock National Site
2- Capital: Lincoln
1- Largest city: Omaha

(Nebraska)

5- Silver producing state
4- Hoover Dam
3- Lake Tahoe
2- Capital: Carson City
1- Abbreviation: NV

(Nevada)

5- A New England state
4- First to vote for Declaration of Independence
3- Home of Daniel Webster
2- Capital: Concord
1- Abbreviation: NH

(New Hampshire)

5- Third state to enter the union
4- Princeton University
3- Famous city: Atlantic City
2- Capital: Trenton
1- Abbreviation: NJ

(New Jersey)

5- Has large areas of desert
4- Los Alamos: site of first atomic bomb test
3- White Sands National Monument
2- Largest city: Albuquerque
1- Capital: Santa Fe

(New Mexico)

5- Niagara Falls on U.S.-Canada border
4- Baseball Hall of Fame
3- Home of 3 Presidents: Martin Van Buren, Franklin Roosevelt, Theodore Roosevelt
2- Capital: Albany
1- Has largest U.S. city

(New York)

5- Great Smoky Mountain National Park
4- First air flight took place in this state
3- Cape Hatteras is off its coast
2- Largest city: Charlotte
1- Capital: Raleigh

(North Carolina)

5- Most rural state; 90% farms
4- International Peace Park
3- West of Minnesota
2- Largest city: Fargo
1- Capital: Bismarck

(North Dakota)

5- Pro Football Hall of Fame
4- Home of 5 Presidents: Grant, Taft, Hayes, Harding, Garfield
3- Bordered on the north by Lake Erie
2- Nickname: Buckeye State
1- Largest City: Cleveland

(Ohio)

5- Rich in oil fields
4- National Cowboy Hall of Fame
3- Will Rogers Memorial
2- Shaped like a pot with handle
1- Abbreviation: OK

(Oklahoma)

5- Crater Lake, deepest U.S. lake
4- Mount Hood and Cascade Mountains
3- Largest city: Portland
2- On northern border is Columbia River
1- Capital: Salem

(Oregon)

5- Home of Benjamin Franklin
4- Valley Forge National Park
3- Gettysburg National Park
2- Liberty Bell
1- Largest city: Philadelphia

(Pennsylvania)

5- First in production of jewelry and silverware
4- Founded by Roger Williams
3- A New England State
2- Capital: Providence
1- Smallest of the 50 states

(Rhode Island)

5- Civil War started here
4- Many old plantations
3- Grows more peaches than any other state except California
2- Capital: Columbia
1- Abbreviation: SC

(South Carolina)

5- Black Hills
4- "Wild Bill" Hickok killed in Deadwood
3- Badlands
2- Capital: Pierre
1- Mount Rushmore

(South Dakota)

5- The Hermitage, home of President Andrew Jackson
4- Museum of Atomic Energy at Oak Ridge
3- Great Smoky Mountain National Park
2- Largest city: Memphis
1- Capital: Nashville

(Tennessee)

5- Headquarters of NASA
4- First in oil production
3- Home of President Lyndon Johnson
2- The Alamo
1- Largest city: Houston

(Texas)

5- Bryce Canyon and Zion National Parks
4- Rainbow Bridge
3- Mormon Tabernacle
2- Great Salt Lake
1- Capital: Salt Lake City

(Utah)

5- First state after original 13 to join the union
4- First in producing maple syrup
3- Home of President Calvin Coolidge
2- Capital: Montpelier
1- Abbreviation: VT

(Vermont)

5- Surrender sites of both American Revolution and Civil War
4- Home of Washington and seven other presidents
3- Arlington National Cemetery
2- Shenandoah National Park
1- Capital: Richmond

(Virginia)

5- First in production of apples
4- Mount St. Helens erupted here in 1980
3- Space Needle
2- Bordered on the south by the Columbia River
1- Largest city: Seattle

(Washington)

5- Harper's Ferry
4- Part of another state until the Civil War
3- Nickname: Mountain State
2- Capital: Charleston
1- Abbreviation: WV

(West Virginia)

5- First in production of milk and cheese
4- Largest Lake: Lake Winnebago
3- Bordered on the east by Lake Michigan
2- Capital: Madison
1- Largest city: Milwaukee

(Wisconsin)

5- Grand Teton Mountains
4- Devil's Tower National Monument
3- Capital: Laramie
2- Yellowstone National Park
1- Abbreviation: WY

(Wyoming)

What State Are You In?

Each card in this game names a major city in the United States that is not a state capital. Players earn points by naming the state in which each city is found.

Purpose: to practice and review knowledge of major U.S. cities

Materials Needed:

- card stock of any color to print game cards and to mount rules and answer key
- laminating materials

Construction:

1. Print game card pages on colored card stock. Laminate pages, then cut cards apart.
2. Trim rules box and answer key box. Mount them on the same color card stock as used for the game cards and laminate them.

Rules for "What State Are You In?"

This game is for two to three players and one scorekeeper. Paper and pencil are needed for keeping score. Players sit so that all may see the card. Scorekeeper sits opposite the players and holds the answer key.

1. Scorekeeper shuffles the cards and places them face down.

2. Scorekeeper turns first card up and places it in front of players.

3. If a player knows the state in which the city is found, player quietly places a hand over the card and says its name.

4. Scorekeeper checks the answer key and scores as follows:

   Correct answer: Win 2 points. Card goes to discard pile.

   Incorrect answer: Lose 2 points. Card goes to bottom of pile.

5. When all the cards are used or when game time is over, the player with the most points is the winner.

---

1. ALBUQUERQUE	2. BALTIMORE	3. BUFFALO
4. CHARLOTTE	5. CHICAGO	6. CINCINNATI
7. CLEVELAND	8. DALLAS	9. DETROIT
10. EL PASO	11. FORT WORTH	12. HOUSTON
13. JACKSONVILLE	14. KANSAS CITY	15. LOS ANGELES

16. MEMPHIS	**17.** MIAMI	**18.** MILWAUKEE
19. MINNEAPOLIS	**20.** NEWARK	**21.** NEW ORLEANS
22. NEW YORK	**23.** OMAHA	**24.** PHILADELPHIA
25. PITTSBURGH	**26.** PORTLAND	**27.** ST. LOUIS
28. SAN ANTONIO	**29.** SAN DIEGO	**30.** SAN FRANCISCO

31. SEATTLE	32. TOLEDO	33. TUCSON
34. TULSA	35. ORLANDO	36. TAMPA
37. BIRMINGHAM	38. CHATTANOOGA	39. RENO
40. LAS VEGAS	41. FLAGSTAFF	42. TACOMA

Answer Key for "What State Are You In?"

1. New Mexico
2. Maryland
3. New York
4. North Carolina
5. Illinois
6. Ohio
7. Ohio
8. Texas
9. Michigan
10. Texas
11. Texas
12. Texas
13. Florida
14. Missouri or Kansas
15. California
16. Tennessee
17. Florida
18. Wisconsin
19. Minnesota
20. New Jersey
21. Louisiana
22. New York
23. Nebraska
24. Pennsylvania
25. Pennsylvania
26. Oregon or Maine
27. Missouri
28. Texas
29. California
30. California
31. Washington
32. Ohio
33. Arizona
34. Oklahoma
35. Florida
36. Florida
37. Alabama
38. Tennessee
39. Nevada
40. Nevada
41. Arizona
42. Washington

Find the State

This game is challenging. Each card in this game has a sentence with a state name hidden somewhere within it. Players earn points for locating the hidden state names.

Purpose: to analyze data to find the hidden name of a state.

Materials Needed:

- card stock of any color to print game cards and to mount rules and answer key
- laminating materials

Construction:

1. Print game card pages on colored card stock. Laminate pages, then cut cards apart.
2. Trim rules box and answer key box. Mount them on the same color of card stock as used for the game cards and laminate them.

Rules for "Find the State"

This game is for two players and one scorekeeper. Paper and pencil are needed for keeping score. Players sit side-by-side so that both may see the game card. Scorekeeper sits opposite the players.

1. Scorekeeper shuffles the cards and places them face down.
2. Scorekeeper turns first card up and places it in front of players.
3. If a player finds the state name hidden in the sentence, the player quietly places a hand over the card and names the state.
4. Scorekeeper checks answer key and scores as follows:

   Correct answer: Win 2 points. Card goes to discard pile.

   Incorrect answer: Lose 2 points. Card goes to bottom of pile.

5. Players can earn two additional points by naming the capital of the state hidden in the sentence. They do not lose points for incorrect answer.
6. When all cards are used or when game time is over, the player with the most points is the winner.

1.

In parts of India, natives get used to very hot, dry weather.

2.

Billy yelled, "Ma, I need some money for this week."

3.

Since we moved, I really do miss our indoor swimming pool.

4.

The telegram read, "Vein exhausted. Ore Gone. Closing mine."

5.

The art assignment is to draw and color a doll, a book, and a kite.

6.

O, hi, Oscar! I didn't know you were coming to the party.

7.

When Cassio was at the circus, he got the clown's autograph.

8.

When Eva darted into the street, she almost got hit by a car.

9.

Louise and her mother chose shirts in three colors: lemon, tan, and grape.

10.

The banker's advice was, "Pay your bills weekly—never monthly."

11.

In a little town named Belflor, I dated a girl named Flora.

12.

Carl has three jobs: he works in a lab, a machine shop, and a drugstore.

13.

Is Tex most admired for his courage or giant strength?

14.

Here is the report, Louis; I analyzed the information carefully before I wrote it.

15.

On Main Street, go south, Carol. In a few minutes you will come to the book store.

16.

Mark Wilkans asked Cal Isman for directions to the mechanics shop.

17.

I knew Hamp's hired delivery man was quitting so I applied for the job.

18.

That cute little miss is sipping her lemonade daintily.

19.

Mr. Carl Rhode is landing at O'Hare Airport at two o'clock; please meet his plane.

20.

The Miami, Chigano, and Shewa Indian tribes once lived in heavily forested regions of the south.

21.

Mark an' Sassy have been goin' steady for two years.

22.

There is cake left, Minne, so take some home to Micke.

23.

We went to the fair because we knew jersey cows and black angus were being shown in the competition.

24.

Hey, Lewis, Con's in the library waiting for you to study with him.

25.

Della knew Yorkshire puppies were expensive but she wanted one anyway.

26.

Let's fix these wires. You connect, I cut off excess. Okay?

27.

When I was ill, I noisily coughed and huskily cleared my throat.

28.

I saw them driving north, Carol in a convertible and Michael in a truck.

29.

Did you see Ken Tucker and Mary Landers at the 8 o'clock movie?

30.

You will cut a hand if you pick up the knife carelessly.

31.

Please, Ken, tuck your shirt in before you leave for school.

32.

Dad said, "A hoe is in the barn. Will you get it for me?"

33.

You must do the washing tonight if you are going to have clean clothes for school tomorrow.

34.

Matt, exasperate is a synonym for irritate or annoy.

35.

Penn, Syl, Van, I, and you are sitting together at the banquet.

36.

Wynn bragged, "She's my gal, ask any person in this school."

Answer Key for "Find the State"

1. Indiana, Indianapolis

2. Maine, Augusta

3. Missouri, Jefferson City

4. Oregon, Salem

5. Colorado, Denver

6. Ohio, Columbus

7. Iowa, Des Moines

8. Nevada, Carson City

9. Montana, Helena

10. Vermont, Montpelier

11. Florida, Tallahassee

12. Alabama, Montgomery

13. Georgia, Atlanta

14. Louisiana, Baton Rouge

15. South Carolina, Columbia

16. Kansas, Topeka

17. New Hampshire, Concord

18. Mississippi, Jackson

19. Rhode Island, Providence

20. Michigan, Lansing

21. Arkansas, Little Rock

22. Minnesota, Minneapolis

23. New Jersey, Trenton

24. Wisconsin, Milwaukee

25. New York, Albany

26. Connecticut, Hartford

27. Illinois, Springfield

28. North Carolina, Raleigh

29. Maryland, Annapolis

30. Utah, Salt Lake City

31. Kentucky, Frankfort

32. Idaho, Boise

33. Washington, Olympia

34. Texas, Austin

35. Pennsylvania, Harrisburg

36. Alaska, Juneau

Geography Genius

This game has 140 questions about land formations and bodies of water. The game can be played simultaneously by four or five groups or with the entire class at once as a team competition. If students play in small groups, be sure to give each group an equal number of game cards and its own copy of the rules and the answer key.

Purpose: to review vocabulary on world geography

Materials Needed:

- card stock of any color to print game cards and to mount rules and answer key
- laminating materials

Construction:

1. Print game card pages on colored card stock. Laminate pages, then cut cards apart.

2. Trim rules box and answer key box. Mount them on the same color of card stock as used for the game cards and laminate them. **Note:** If several groups are to play at the same time, make enough copies of the rules and the answer key so that each group has its own rule box and answer key.

    Rules for "Geography Genius"

This game is for three or four players and one judge.

1. Judge shuffles the cards and spreads them face down on the table.

2. Player to judge's left goes first.

3. First player takes a card, reads aloud the card number and question, and answers the question.

4. Judge checks answer from the answer key.

5. Players earn points by keeping cards for questions they have answered correctly. When a player answers a question incorrectly, the card is shuffled back into the card pile to be used again.

6. When game time is over or when all cards have been used, players count their cards. The player with the most cards is the winner.

7. If there is time, shuffle the cards and play again or trade cards with another group to play with different questions.

1.

A man-made channel filled with water and used for boat transportation or for irrigation is called a _____.

2.

A deep, narrow gorge with high, steep sides that has been cut by running water is called a _____.

3.

A word meaning elevation or height above sea level is _____.

4.

The entire area that is drained by a large river is called a _____ _____.

5.

What word refers to a bay, cove, or other recess along the coast?

6.

What do we call the part of a river where it empties into a large body of water?

7.

An area of land that gets very little rainfall and has little plant life is called a _____.

8.

When a river empties into a larger body of water, it forms a triangle-shaped area of mud, sand, and silt known as a _____.

9.

When we measure the degree of hotness or coldness of an environment, we are measuring the _____.

10.

Moisture that falls from the clouds as sleet, rain, snow, or hail is known as _____.

11.

A small river that flows into a larger one is called a _____.

12.

A stream or other body of water where a river begins is called the river's _____.

13.

What landform is completely surrounded by water?

14.

What landform is surrounded by water on three sides?

15.

The periodic rise and fall of the water level of the ocean is called the _____.

16.

The rise and fall of the tide is caused by the gravitational pull of the _____.

17.

The point on a mountain above which there is snow all year round is called the _____ _____.

18.

What word is defined as a narrow passageway of water that connects two large bodies of water?

19.

What do we call the highest point of a hill or a mountain?

20.

A _____ is a large stream of water of natural origin which drains an area of land and empties into another body of water.

21.

Low, spongy ground that is too wet for farming, but has abundant plant and animal life is called a _____.

22.

The point on a mountain above which no trees will grow because of the cold temperature is called the _____ _____.

23.

The average level of the ocean's surface as measured along the shoreline is known as _____ _____.

24.

A flat, elevated region of land is known as tableland or a _____.

25.

Useful materials that are found in nature such as water, minerals, and trees are called _____ _____.

26.

A small, still body of water that is smaller than a lake is called a _____.

27.

The vast area of natural grassland in the middle part of the United States is called the _____.

28.

The part of a river or stream where the water flows swiftly over rocks is called the _____.

29.

A cone-shaped mountain formed by eruption of molten rock, cinders and steam is called a _____.

30.

What is the general term for all growing plants?

31.

A _____ is a bank beside a stream or river created to prevent flooding.

32.

Imaginary lines that are used to help locate places and objects are called lines of _____ and _____.

33.

What is the imaginary line that divides the Northern Hemisphere from the Southern Hemisphere?

34.

A very large ocean inlet such as the one that separates Florida from Mexico is called a _____.

35.

The wearing away of soil and rock by wind and water is called _____.

36.

When someone recycles newspapers, cans, and plastic containers, he or she is helping to save natural resources by practicing _____.

37.

A book of maps is called an _____.

38.

The portion of a continent that is submerged beneath the ocean is called the _____ _____.

39.

The bowl-shaped depression at the top of a volcano is called a _____.

40.

The line where the earth and sky seem to meet is called the _____.

41.

A hill or a ridge of sand that is piled up by the wind is called a _____.

42.

A narrow piece of land that joins two larger areas of land is called an _____.

43.

The largest bodies of land on the earth are called _____.

44.

Name the largest continent.

45.

Name the smallest continent.

46.

On which continent is Canada located?

47.

What do we mean when we say the "contiguous" 48 states? Name the two U.S. states that are not "contiguous."

48.

What do we call a person who follows a career of mapmaking?

49.

Name the "grand" natural site in the western U.S. where the Colorado River flows.

50.

This large lake in the western U.S. has no outlet, loses water only through evaporation, and is called the _____ _____ _____.

51.

On which of the Hawaiian Islands is the capital city of Honolulu located?

52.

Name the largest island in the Hawaiian Islands group.

53.

Name the longest river in the U.S.

54.

Name the Great Lakes.

55.

The lowest place in the U.S. is in California. Name this valley.

56.

What American desert is located in Southern California?

57.

The deepest lake in the U.S. is almost 2,000 feet deep. It is in Oregon. Name this lake.

58.

The place in the world which receives the most rain is in the U.S. state of _____.

59.

On the east the U.S. is bordered by an ocean. On the west the U.S. is bordered by an ocean. Name these oceans.

60.

New York City, the largest city in the U.S., is located at the mouth of what river?

61.

The world's second largest country is located in North America. Name this country.

62.

The world's second largest lake is in North America. Name this lake.

63.

The second largest lake in the world is Lake Superior. What two countries border on this lake?

64.

What famous waterfall is located on the river that connects Lake Erie and Lake Ontario?

65.

If one travels across the Great Lakes from west to east, on which lake will one begin the trip?

66.

All of the 48 contiguous states border at least two other states except for one. Name this state that borders only one other U.S. state.

67.

The U.S. is divided into 50 states. Canada is divided into two territories and ten _____.

68.

What large U.S. river flows east and empties into the Mississippi River at St. Louis, Missouri?

69.

Name the seaway that connects the Great Lakes with the Atlantic Ocean.

70.

The city of Chicago is located on the shore of what body of water?

71.

What major U.S. river flows west and empties into the Mississippi River at Cairo, Illinois?

72.

The Rocky Mountain ridge that separates rivers that flow west to the Pacific and rivers that flow east to the Atlantic is called the _____ _____.

73.

Which Great Lake is the smallest in length and width?

74.

The best-known swamp in the U.S. is a national park in Florida. Name this swamp.

75.

Which U.S. state has a coastline on both the Atlantic Ocean and the Gulf of Mexico?

76.

Which mountain chain in the United States has the highest mountains—the Rocky Mountains or the Appalachian Mountains?

77.

Name the river that separates Texas from Mexico.

78.

What large body of water is bordered by Texas, Louisiana, Mississippi, Alabama, and Florida?

79.

What large island is located approximately 200 miles from Miami, Florida?

80.

Which of these California cities is closest to the Mexican border: Los Angeles, San Francisco, or San Diego?

81.

The Yucatan is a land area of Mexico. Is the Yucatan a mountain, a desert, or a peninsula?

82.

Baja California is a long, narrow peninsula that is part of Mexico. What U.S. state borders this peninsula on its north?

83.

If you were visiting the states of Sonora and Chihuahua, you would be in what country?

84.

The people of Mexico and other countries of Central America speak what language?

85.

What is the capital of Mexico?

86.

If you fly due south from New York City and you land in Brazil, on what continent will you be standing?

87.

The second longest river of the world is in South America. Name this river.

88.

Which country of South America has the largest area?

89.

Which country of South America is the second largest in area?

90.

Name the very high mountain range that runs 4,000 miles down the west coast of South America.

91.

What animal found in South America's Andes Mountains has been tamed to carry both people and materials?

92.

The world's largest waterfall is Angel Falls. Name the country and continent where you would go to see this famous waterfall.

93.

The world's highest city is 9,343 feet above sea level and is the capital of Ecuador in South America. Name this capital city.

94.

The driest place in the world is the Atacama Desert in a long, narrow South American country that borders Argentina. Name this country.

95.

If you left South America and sailed east along the equator, you would come to what continent?

96.

The longest river in the world is the _____ River on the continent of _____.

97.

The highest mountain in Africa is in Tanzania. Name this mountain.

98.

The largest city in Africa is the capital of Egypt. Name this capital city.

99.

Name the large body of water that borders Africa on the north.

100.

Egypt has coastline on what two seas?

101.

Africa is bordered by the _____ Ocean on the west and on the _____ Ocean on the east.

102.

The world's largest desert covers much of Northern Africa. Name this desert.

103.

Name the southernmost country of Africa.

104.

The country of South Africa is well-known for mining what valuable gems?

105.

If you were visiting the African savannah, would you be in a jungle or grassland?

106.

Name the largest country of Africa.

107.

Liberia, a country on the west coast of Africa has a capital city that is named for a U.S. President. Name this city.

108.

Name the long, narrow sea that separates Africa from the Middle East country of Saudi Arabia.

109.

Name the canal that is a passageway between the Mediterranean Sea and the Red Sea.

110.

Name the waterway through which ships pass from the Mediterranean Sea into the Atlantic Ocean.

111.

The Strait of Gibraltar separates the African country of _____ and the European country of _____.

112.

You are traveling by boat from Greece westward to Turkey. What small sea are you crossing?

113.

Which two countries of Europe are separated by the English Channel?

114.

What boot-shaped country of Europe is a peninsula that sticks out into the Mediterranean Sea?

115.

The Iberian Peninsula is surrounded by ocean on three sides. What two European countries make up this peninsula?

116.

In the Norwegian Sea, about halfway between Norway and Greenland, is the island nation of _____.

117.

The two most well-known cities of Europe are _____, the capital of England, and _____, the capital of France.

118.

Iceland, a large island in the North Atlantic Ocean is a part of what continent?

119.

Name the three countries that make up the area known as Scandinavia.

120.

Name the four countries that make up the area known as Great Britain.

121.

What mountains separate Europe from Asia?

122.

What ocean lies to the south of Asia?

123.

The largest country in Asia is also the largest country in the world. Name this country.

124.

Name the second largest country of Asia.

125.

What large desert lies in northern China and southern Mongolia?

126.

Name the large sea that borders Turkey on its north.

127.

The world's highest mountain is in Asia. Name this mountain.

128.

The world's largest city in terms of population is _____, located in the small island nation of _____.

129.

What large gulf separates Saudi Arabia from Iran?

130.

Name the large country of southern Asia that is bordered on the east by the Bay of Bengal and on the west by the Arabian Sea.

131.

Mount Everest, the world's highest mountain, is in what Asian mountain chain?

132.

Name the capital of India.

133.

Name the capital of Russia.

134.

Name the capital of China.

135.

Name the capital of Japan.

136.

What is Japan's largest island?

137.

The Asian country of _____ has more people than any other country in the world.

138.

What name is often used to refer to Europe and Asia together?

139.

The Caspian Sea is bordered on three sides by Russia. What Asian country borders the Caspian Sea on the south?

140.

The Philippines is a country made up of a group of islands lying southeast of China. Name the capital of this island country.

Answer Key for "Geography Genius"

1. Canal
2. Canyon
3. Altitude
4. River system
5. Inlet
6. Mouth
7. Desert
8. Delta
9. Temperature
10. Precipitation
11. Tributary
12. Source
13. Island
14. Peninsula
15. Tide
16. Moon
17. Snow line
18. Strait
19. Summit or peak
20. River
21. Swamp
22. Tree line
23. Sea level
24. Mesa or plateau
25. Natural resources
26. Pond
27. Prairie
28. Rapids
29. Volcano
30. Flora or vegetation
31. Levee
32. Latitude; longitude
33. Equator
34. Gulf
35. Erosion
36. Conservation
37. Atlas
38. Continental shelf
39. Crater
40. Horizon
41. Dune
42. Isthmus
43. Continents
44. Asia
45. Australia
46. North America
47. States that touch each other; Alaska, Hawaii
48. Cartographer
49. Grand Canyon
50. Great Salt Lake
51. Oahu
52. Hawaii
53. Mississippi River
54. Huron; Ontario; Michigan; Erie; Superior
55. Death Valley
56. Mojave Desert
57. Crater Lake
58. Hawaii
59. Atlantic; Pacific
60. Hudson River
61. Canada
62. Lake Superior
63. Canada; United States
64. Niagara Falls
65. Lake Superior
66. Maine
67. Provinces
68. Missouri River
69. St. Lawrence Seaway
70. Lake Michigan

Answer Key for "Geography Genius" *(cont.)*

71. Ohio River
72. Continental Divide
73. Lake Ontario
74. Everglades
75. Florida
76. Rocky Mountains
77. Rio Grande
78. Gulf of Mexico
79. Cuba
80. San Diego
81. Peninsula
82. California
83. Mexico
84. Spanish
85. Mexico City
86. South America
87. Amazon River
88. Brazil
89. Argentina
90. Andes Mountains
91. Llama
92. Venezuela; South America
93. Quito
94. Chile
95. Africa
96. Nile; Africa
97. Mount Kilimanjaro
98. Cairo
99. Mediterranean Sea
100. Mediterranean Sea; Red Sea
101. Atlantic; Indian
102. Sahara Desert
103. South Africa
104. Diamonds
105. Grassland

106. Sudan
107. Monrovia (named for James Monroe)
108. Red Sea
109. Suez Canal
110. Strait of Gibraltar
111. Morocco; Spain
112. Aegean Sea
113. France; England
114. Italy
115. Portugal and Spain
116. Iceland
117. London; Paris
118. Europe
119. Norway; Sweden; Finland
120. England; Scotland; Ireland; Wales
121. Ural Mountains
122. Indian Ocean
123. Russia
124. China
125. Gobi Desert
126. Black Sea
127. Mount Everest
128. Tokyo; Japan
129. Persian Gulf
130. India
131. Himalayan Mountains
132. New Delhi
133. Moscow
134. Beijing (formerly Peking)
135. Tokyo
136. Honshu
137. China
138. Eurasia
139. Iran
140. Manila

Our Colorful World

What a colorful world we live in! This game has 90 questions about colorful people, places, and things. The game can be played in one of three ways: in three small groups, giving 30 cards to each group; as team competition in which the whole class participates; or simply with the entire class. Your students will be surprised at how many things in our world are identified by color.

Purpose: to identify people, places, and things with colorful names

Materials Needed:

- card stock of any color to print game cards and to mount rules
- laminating materials

Construction:

1. Print the game card pages on colored card stock. Laminate pages, then cut cards apart.
2. Trim the rules box. Mount it on the same color of card stock as used for the game cards and laminate it. **Note:** If the game is to be played by 3 groups at one time, make a copy of the rules for each group.

Rules for "Our Colorful World"

This game is for three or four players and one scorekeeper. Pencil and paper are needed for keeping score.

1. Scorekeeper shuffles the cards and places them face down.

2. Scorekeeper picks up the first card and reads the question to the player on his or her left.

3. Scorekeeper keeps score as follows:

   Correct answer: Win 2 points. Card goes to discard pile. Play continues to the left.

   Incorrect answer: Lose 2 points. Card goes to bottom of deck. Play continues to the left.

4. When all cards are used or when game time is over, the scorekeeper adds the points. Player with the most points is the winner.

Three Indian tribes lived on the plains of Montana in the early 19th century. They were buffalo hunters and tepee dwellers. These tribes were known as the _____ foot Native Americans.

(Black)

Name the band of soldiers led by Ethan Allen during the American Revolution.

(Green Mountain Boys)

In American history, a set of laws listed stores that could not open and things that could not be sold on Sunday. What were these laws called?

(Blue laws)

Name an organization that helps people in times of disaster. It was founded in 1882 by Clara Barton.

(American Red Cross)

During the Civil War, the U.S. government issued paper money that had no backing except the people's trust in the government. What was this money called?

(Greenbacks)

Name the residence that is home to the U.S. president while he is in office.

(White House)

What colorful nickname is sometimes given to a person in the U.S. Navy?

(Blue jacket)

Name the man who led a famous raid on a federal arsenal at Harper's Ferry, West Virginia, in order to get arms to use in the fight against slavery.

(John Brown)

In every town of the Old West there was a man who worked at a forge with his hammer and anvil to make horseshoes and tools. Who was this man?

(Blacksmith)

The _____ and the _____ were words used to refer to troops of the North and South during the Civil War because of their uniform colors.

(Blue; Gray)

In the 1920's and 1930's, workers were often required to sign contracts to say that they were not members of a labor union. What were these contracts called?

(Yellow dog contracts)

Besides being a great patriot, Paul Revere created beautiful metal objects such as tea sets and candlesticks. What was this job called?

(Silversmith)

What is Kentucky's colorful nickname?

(Bluegrass State)

Part of the Appalachian Mountains is a "colorful" range that runs from northern Virginia to northern Georgia. Name this mountain range.

(Blue Ridge Mountains)

It is a crime to threaten to give information to the public unless you are given money. This crime is called _____.

(Blackmail)

What emblem does a person or group display as a sign of surrender?

(White flag)

The state tree of California is a giant known as the _____ tree.

(Redwood)

What does the military call the warning of a coming enemy attack?

(Red alert)

A cowardly person is sometimes described as having a _____ streak.

(Yellow)

On May 10, 1869, the transcontinental railroad was completed with the driving of the _____ at Ogden, Utah.

(Golden Spike)

Vermont gained a nickname because of a mountain chain in that state. What is Vermont's nickname?

(Green Mountain State)

Name the first national park created in the U.S.

(Yellowstone National Park)

You are in South Dakota. You have come to see the famous _____ Hills.

(Black)

Each year the White House Christmas tree is set up in which colorful room?

(Blue Room)

Name the colorful bird that is the state bird of 4 states: Idaho, Missouri, Nevada, and New York.

(Blue Bird)

When someone has many debts, he or she is said to be in the _____.

(Red)

Someone who is new on the job or lacks experience is called _____.

(Green)

A person with a special talent for growing plants is said to have a _____ _____.

(Green thumb)

Three states—Illinois, New Jersey, and Rhode Island—have named the _____ as their state flower.

(Violet)

Name the colorful bird that is the state bird for seven states.

(Cardinal or redbird)

A photographic print of building plans is called a _____.

(Blueprint)

Name a poisonous spider found in the American southwest.

(Black widow)

Name the professional football team that plays in Washington, D.C.

(Washington Redskins)

Name a wildflower of the Midwest that is also the state flower of Maryland.

(Black-eyed Susan)

Name a river that starts in West Texas and crosses Louisiana to empty into the Mississippi.

(Red River)

The U.S. flag is commonly referred to as the _____, _____, and _____.

(Red, white, and blue)

A colorful song often sung in the state of Texas is "The _____ _____ of Texas."

(Yellow Rose)

U.S. Army uniforms are sometimes called "o.d."s What does "o.d." stand for?

(Olive drab)

Name a professional football team that plays in Wisconsin.

(Green Bay Packers)

You are in Colorado. You have come to visit the _____ Canyon of the Gunnison.

(Black)

Someone caught in the act of wrong-doing is said to be caught _____.

(Red-handed)

Official forms and procedures that are difficult and time-consuming are said to be full of _____ _____.

(Red tape)

You want to find the phone numbers of several businesses in town. What source will you use?

(The Yellow Pages)

When a foreign dignitary visits the United States, he or she receives the _____ _____ treatment.

(Red carpet)

When someone commits a terrible error, he or she may become _____ _____ _____ _____.

(Red as a beet)

What colorful expression is used to refer to a very special day?

(Red letter day)

Something that happens very rarely is said to happen only _____ _____ _____ _____ _____.

(Once in a blue moon)

What "shiny" nickname does the state of Nevada have?

(Silver State)

There is a popular tourist attraction near Branson, Missouri, called _____ _____ _____.

(Silver Dollar City)

Florida's state flower is sometimes used as a wedding decoration. What is this fragrant white blossom?

(Orange blossom)

What "shiny" nickname does the state of California have?

(Golden state)

What 1848 discovery at Sutter's Mill in California led to a great rush of settlers to that area?

(Gold)

What colorful bridge is located in San Francisco, California?

(Golden Gate Bridge)

In New Mexico, you can see the largest gypsum deposit in the world. It is called the _____ _____ National Monument.

(White Sands)

Our neighboring country to the north has a large maple leaf centered on its national flag. What color is this maple leaf?

(Red)

As an American tourist you have decided to visit the Middle East. What sea will you visit that is west of Saudi Arabia?

(Red Sea)

As an American tourist you are visiting Turkey. You will spend a few days on Turkey's northern border visiting the _____ Sea.

(Black)

You are visiting South Korea and will cross the _____ Sea to travel to Beijing, China.

(Yellow)

You are an American tourist visiting Ireland where you discover that one of Ireland's nicknames is quite colorful. What is this colorful nickname?

(Emerald Isle)

In 1865, American author Mary Mapes Dodge wrote the children's classic, *Hans Brinker*, about a Dutch boy and his prize possession. What was this colorful prize possession?

(Silver skates)

Wage earning workers who wear uniforms and do manual labor are often called _____ _____ _____.

(Blue collar workers)

Professional workers whose jobs do not generally involve manual labor are often called _____ _____ _____.

(White collar workers)

Name a colorful flowering tree often seen growing in the wild or used in landscaping. It is Oklahoma's state tree.

(Redbud)

You are in Utah. You have come to see the world's largest natural bridge. In its sandstone you can see many colors. Name this natural bridge.

(Rainbow Bridge)

You are in Dearborn, Michigan. You are visiting a reconstructed village typical of 19th century America. What popular tourist site are you visiting?

(Greenfield Village)

American author Stephen Crane gained fame in 1895 when he wrote a book about a young boy's experiences in the Civil War. What is the title of this book?

(Red Badge of Courage)

What is the award for a first place win in the Olympics?

(A gold medal)

What is the award for a second place win in the Olympics?

(A silver medal)

What is the award for a third place win in the Olympics?

(A bronze medal)

The _____ River begins in northwest Arkansas and flows southeast to empty into the Mississippi.

(White)

Your parent goes to a _____ sale to buy sheets, pillowcases, and other linens for your family.

(White)

You have entered a calf in competition at the state fair and your calf has won first place. What kind of award will you probably receive?

(Blue ribbon)

The list of people that clubs or organizations do not wish to become members is known as a _____ list.

(Black)

What is the name of the woman who became America's first female doctor?

(Elizabeth Blackwell)

There are four ranks in judo, each recognized by awarding a colorful belt. What belt is awarded at the highest rank?

(Black belt)

You are visiting Africa. One of the places you want to see is the spot where two rivers join to form the Nile River. Name these two rivers.

(Blue Nile and White Nile)

The first American astronaut to walk in space was Edward H. _____.

(White)

American astronauts have a wonderful view of earth when they are in space. They have often said that, from space, the earth looks like a big _____ _____.

(Blue marble)

A false clue or a diversion meant to take attention away from the real issue is called a _____ _____.

(Red herring)

What term is used to describe illegal trade in goods?

(Black market)

Because of their uniforms, British soldiers who fought in the American Revolution were given what colorful nickname?

(Redcoats)

The Homestake Mine is located in the Black Hills of South Dakota. It is the largest _____ mine in the U.S.

(Gold)

When someone is easily taken in by an empty promise, people often say, "All that glitters is not _____."

(Gold)

You are going on a ski trip to the highest mountains in New England. You will be in northern New Hampshire. What mountains will you be visiting?

(White Mountains)

One of the most popular novels in American literature is *Gone with the Wind*. What is the name of this novel's heroine?

(Scarlett O'Hara)

Superstition says that you will have good luck all year long if you eat _____ _____ on New Year's Day.

(Black-eyed peas)

Tradition says that on her wedding day a bride should wear something borrowed and something _____.

(Blue)

When someone gets bad news, people often say, "Every cloud has a _____ lining."

(Silver)

Newspaper reporting that uses misleading information and distorted pictures to attract readers is called _____ journalism.

(Yellow)

Slow jazz songs about lost love, poverty and hard work are known as the _____.

(Blues)

Traveling Songs

Each card in this game names a song title containing a place such as a city, state, or country. Most places are located in the United States, but some songs refer to other countries. After naming the place that belongs in the title, the player is then asked a question about it.

Even though many of these song titles will be unfamiliar to students, this game provides a good way to offer exposure to music of past years and practice geography at the same time. To make the game more fun, play recordings of some of the songs to familiarize students with them.

Purpose: to practice geographical knowledge and learn the titles of old-time songs

Materials Needed:

- card stock of any color to print game cards and to mount rules and answer key
- laminating materials

Construction:

1. Print the game card pages on colored card stock. Laminate the pages, then cut cards apart.
2. Trim the rules and answer key boxes. Mount them on the same color of card stock as used for the game cards and laminate them.

Rules for "Traveling Songs"

This game is for three or four players and one scorekeeper. Pencil and paper are needed for keeping score.

1. Scorekeeper shuffles the cards and spread them face down on the table.
2. Player to the scorekeeper's left goes first. Play moves to the left.
3. First player picks a card and reads the card number and song title aloud.
4. Scorekeeper checks the answer key and scores as follows:

   Correct song title: Win 1 point.

   Correct answer: Win additional point.

   Incorrect answer: Place card in discard pile.

   Play continues to the left.

5. When all cards are used or when game time is over, the scorekeeper adds the points. Player with the most points is the winner.

1.

"Meet Me in _____" (U.S. city)

Name the state in which this Midwestern city is located.

2.

"_____ Here I Come" (state)

What ocean borders this state?

3.

"Back Home Again in _____" (state)

The northwest corner of this state is bordered by which one of the Great Lakes?

4.

"_____ Waltz" (State song of a state that begins with an "M")

Name another state to put in the blank to make the title of another state song.

5.

"_____ Polka" (One of the original 13 states)

This state is named for which famous colonist?

6.

"Carry Me Back to Old _____" (state)

George Washington's home place is in this state. Name this home place.

7.

"April in _____" (Famous world city)

In which country is this city located?

8.

"In Foggy _____ Town" (Famous world city)

In which country is this city located?

9.

"Sidewalks of _____" (U.S. city)

This largest U.S. city is not its state capital. Name the state capital.

10.

"Stars Fell on _____" (state)

A small part of this state's southern border touches what large body of water?

11.

"_____ on My Mind" (state)

The 1996 Summer Olympics were held in this state's capital. Name this capital.

12.

"I Left My Heart in _____" (U.S. city)

This city is known for a famous bridge. Name this well-known bridge.

13.

"Slow Boat to _____" (Far Eastern country)

Name the continent on which this country is located.

14.

"Moonlight in _____" (state)

This state is famous for what product that we sometimes eat with breakfast?

15.

"_____, My _____" (State song of a state that begins with an "M")

This small eastern state is almost cut in half by what bay?

16.

"_____ Choo-Choo" (U.S. city)

This city is in the home state of Al Gore, Vice President to President Bill Clinton. Name the state.

17.

"Way Down Yonder in _____" (U.S. city)

This city, the site of the annual Mardi Gras celebrations, is located in what state?

18.

"My Old _____ Home" (state)

Name this state's capital.

19.

"Shuffle Off to _____" (U.S. city)

This city is located at the northeastern tip of which of the Great Lakes?

20.

"Why, Oh Why, Did I Ever Leave _____?" (state)

This state's largest city is home to the Rock and Roll Hall of Fame. Name this city.

21.

"Yellow Rose of _____" (state)

Name the capital of this second largest state.

22.

"_____ _____, Here I Come" (U.S. city)

This Missouri city has a professional baseball team and a professional football them. Name these 2 teams.

23.

"Blue _____" (state)

This state was the 50th to join the Union. Name the 49th state to enter the Union.

24.

"South of the Border, Down _____ Way" (country)

What is the capital of this country?

25.

"_____ Moon" (two states, either North or South)

Name the capital city of each of these states.

26.

"_____ the Beautiful" (country)

Name this country's neighboring country on the north and neighboring country on the south.

27.

"It's Sweet to Beat Your Feet in the _____ Mud" (river and state)

The long river named in this song empties into what large body of water?

28.

"_____, _____, That Toddling Town" (U.S. city)

Name the state in which this third largest U.S. city is found.

29.

"Did Your Mother Come from _____?" (country)

This country, land of leprechauns and shamrocks, is a part of which continent?

30.

"Blue _____ Waltz" (river—not U.S.)

This river rises in Germany and empties into a sea that is north of Turkey. Name this "colorful" sea.

Answer Key for "Traveling Songs"

1. St. Louis
   Missouri
2. California
   Pacific Ocean
3. Indiana
   Lake Michigan
4. Missouri
   Tennessee
5. Pennsylvania
   William Penn
6. Virginny (Virginia)
   Mount Vernon
7. Paris
   France
8. London
   England
9. New York
   Albany
10. Alabama
    Gulf of Mexico
11. Georgia
    Atlanta
12. San Francisco
    Golden Gate Bridge
13. China
    Asia
14. Vermont
    Maple Syrup
15. Maryland
    Chesapeake Bay

16. Chattanooga
    Tennessee
17. New Orleans
    Louisiana
18. Kentucky
    Frankfort
19. Buffalo
    Lake Erie
20. Ohio
    Cleveland
21. Texas
    Austin
22. Kansas City
    Royals and Chiefs
23. Hawaii
    Alaska
24. Mexico
    Mexico City
25. North Carolina
    Raleigh
    South Carolina
    Columbia
26. America
    Canada
    Mexico
27. Mississippi
    Gulf of Mexico
28. Chicago
    Illinois
29. Ireland
    Europe
30. Danube
    Black Sea

Around the World

This game has 45 cards that name countries of the world. Players must name the continent on which each country is located.

Purpose: to practice and reinforce knowledge of world countries and their continents

Materials Needed:

- card stock of any color to print game card pages and to mount rules and answer key
- laminating materials

Construction:

1. Print the game card pages on colored card stock. Laminate the pages and cut the cards apart.

2. Trim the rules and answer key boxes. Mount on card stock of same color as used for game cards. Laminate them.

Rules for "Around The World"

This game is for two to four players and one scorekeeper. Paper and pencil are needed for keeping score.

1. Scorekeeper shuffles the game cards and spreads cards face down.

2. Player to the left of scorekeeper goes first. Play moves to the left.

3. First player turns over the top card and reads the card number and name of the country aloud. The player attempts to tell the continent on which that country is located.

4. Scorekeeper checks answer key.

   Correct answer: Win 2 points. Card goes to discard pile. Next player's turn.

   Incorrect answer: Lose 2 points. Card is shuffled back into card pile. Next player's turn.

6. When all cards are used or when game time is over, the player with the most points is the winner.

1. ARGENTINA	2. BELGIUM	3. BOLIVIA
4. BRAZIL	5. CANADA	6. CHILE
7. CHINA	8. CUBA	9. EGYPT
10. FRANCE	11. GERMANY	12. GREECE
13. INDIA	14. IRAN	15. IRAQ

16. ISRAEL	17. IRELAND	18. ENGLAND
19. ITALY	20. JAPAN	21. KENYA
22. NORTH KOREA	23. SOUTH KOREA	24. KUWAIT
25. LIBYA	26. MADAGASCAR	27. NETHERLANDS
28. NEW ZEALAND	29. NICARAGUA	30. NIGERIA

31. NORWAY	32. PAKISTAN	33. PERU
34. PHILIPPINES	35. POLAND	36. PORTUGAL
37. SAUDI ARABIA	38. RUSSIA	39. SPAIN
40. SWEDEN	41. SWITZERLAND	42. SYRIA
43. UNITED STATES	44. TURKEY	45. SCOTLAND

Answer Key for "Around the World"

1. South America
2. Europe
3. South America
4. South America
5. North America
6. South America
7. Asia
8. North America
9. Africa
10. Europe
11. Europe
12. Europe
13. Asia
14. Asia
15. Asia
16. Asia
17. Europe
18. Europe
19. Europe
20. Asia
21. Africa
22. Asia
23. Asia

24. Asia
25. Africa
26. Africa
27. Europe
28. Australia
29. South America
30. Africa
31. Europe
32. Asia
33. South America
34. Asia
35. Europe
36. Europe
37. Asia
38. Asia & Europe
39. Europe
40. Europe
41. Europe
42. Asia
43. North America
44. Asia & Europe
45. Europe

Name that Country!

This game has 45 cards, each naming a world capital. Players must name the country in which the capital is located.

Purpose: to practice and reinforce knowledge of world capitals

Materials Needed:

- card stock of any color to print game card pages and to mount rules and answer key
- laminating materials

Construction:

1. Print the game card pages on colored card stock. Laminate the pages and cut the cards apart.

2. Trim the rules and answer key boxes. Mount on card stock of same color as used for game card. Laminate them.

Rules for "Name that Country!"

This game is for two to three players and one scorekeeper. Paper and pencil are needed for keeping score. Players sit so that all may see the card. Scorekeeper sits opposite the players and holds the answer key.

1. Scorekeeper shuffles the cards and places them face down.

2. Scorekeeper turns first card up and places it in front of players.

3. If a player knows the country in which the city is found, quietly place a hand over the card and say its name.

4. Scorekeeper checks the answer key and scores as follows:

   Correct answer: Win 2 points. Card goes to discard pile.

   Incorrect answer: Lose 2 points. Card goes to bottom of pile.

5. The winner is the player who ends up with the most points when all the games are used.

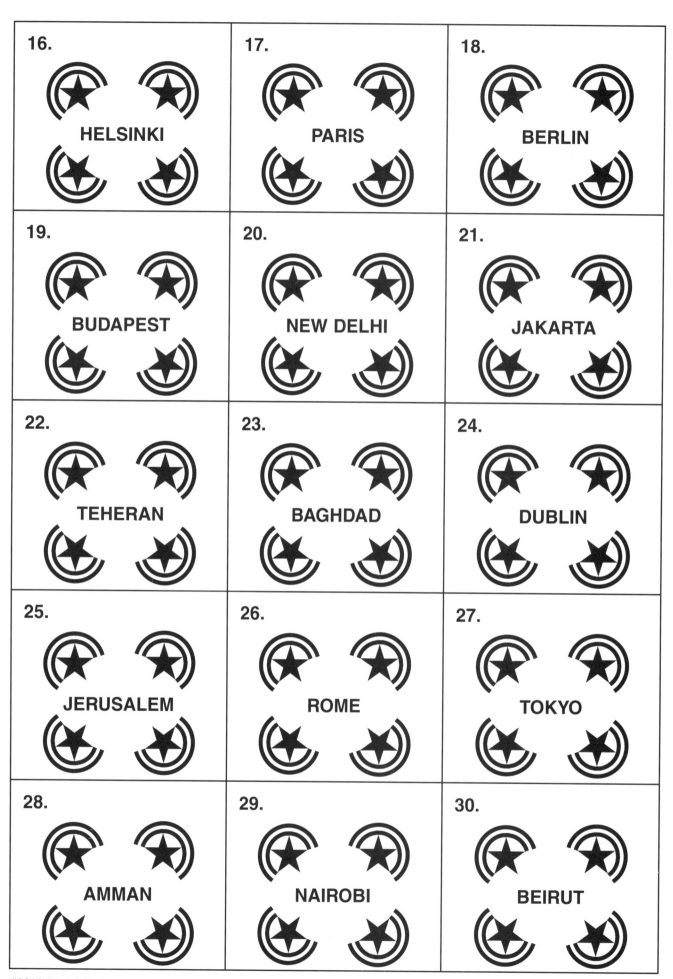

31. WELLINGTON

32. MANAGUA

33. MANILA

34. WARSAW

35. LISBON

36. RIYADH

37. MADRID

38. STOCKHOLM

39. BERN

40. DAMASCUS

41. LONDON

42. BANGKOK

43. ANKARA

44. WASHINGTON, D.C.

45. EDINBURGH

Answer Key for "Name that Country!"

1. Norway
2. Peru
3. Greece
4. Iceland
5. Mexico
6. Russia
7. China
8. Brazil
9. Argentina
10. Australia
11. Canada
12. Chile
13. Cuba
14. Denmark
15. Egypt
16. Finland
17. France
18. Germany
19. Hungary
20. India
21. Indonesia
22. Iran
23. Iraq

24. Ireland
25. Israel
26. Italy
27. Japan
28. Jordan
29. Kenya
30. Lebanon
31. New Zealand
32. Nicaragua
33. Philippines
34. Poland
35. Portugal
36. Saudi Arabia
37. Spain
38. Sweden
39. Switzerland
40. Syria
41. England
42. Thailand
43. Turkey
44. United States
45. Scotland

Climb the Pyramid

This game has 70 questions about ancient and modern Egypt.

Purpose: to practice and reinforce knowledge of Egypt

Materials Needed:

- card stock of any color to print game card pages and to mount rules and answer key
- laminating materials

Construction:

1. Print the game card pages on colored card stock. Laminate the pages and cut the cards apart.

2. Trim the rules and answer key boxes. Mount on card stock of same color as used for game card pages. Laminate them.

3. Page 89 has five cards displaying a pyramid. Print these cards on the same color as the rest of the game and laminate them and cut apart.

Rules for "Climb the Pyramid"

This game is for three to four players and one scorekeeper Pencil and paper are needed for keeping score.

1. Scorekeeper shuffles the cards, including the five pyramid cards. Place cards face down.

2. Player to scorekeeper's left goes first. Play moves to the left.

3. First player takes a card and reads the number and question aloud. Player attempts to answer the question. Scorekeeper checks answer key.

4. Scorekeeper checks the answer key and scores as follows:

   Correct answer: Win 2 points. Card goes to a discard pile. Next player's turn.

   Incorrect answer: Lose 2 points. Card is shuffled back into the card pile. Next player's turn.

6. If a pyramid card is found, the player may risk any or all points accumulated on the next question. If the player answers correctly, the number of points risked are added to his or her score. If the answer is incorrect, points risked are deducted.

7. When time is up or when all cards are gone, the player with most points wins.

1.

Egypt's civilization grew so well and lasted so long because of what river?

2.

In which direction does the Nile River flow?

3.

The Nile River empties into what body of water?

4.

The civilization of ancient Egypt lasted how many thousands of years?

5.

The world's oldest stone building is the Step Pyramid. For which pharaoh was the Step Pyramid built?

6.

The kings of ancient Egypt were called _____.

7.

In ancient Egypt one family of kings might rule for a few years or for centuries. A ruling family such as this was called a _____.

8.

Egypt began in about 3,118 B.C. when Upper Egypt and Lower Egypt were united by the man who became the first pharaoh. Name this king.

9.

The great pyramids were built during which one of Egypt's three kingdoms?

10.

How has the climate of Egypt helped to preserve much of its history?

11.

When an Egyptian died, many of his possessions were buried with him. Why?

12.

The land bordering the Nile River is fertile and green. All of the rest of Egypt is what kind of land?

13.

The king of all the Egyptian gods was Re, the god of the _____.

14.

How does the Nile River compare in length with other rivers of the world?

15.

Two small rivers join in Sudan to form the Nile River. Name these two small rivers.

16.

True or false: There is almost no rain in Egypt.

17.

What was the most important crop grown by Egyptian farmers?

18.

What plant did the Egyptians use to build light boats and to make paper?

19.

Money was not used in ancient Egypt. How did people buy things they wanted?

20.

Farmers of ancient Egypt paid taxes by giving a portion of their _____.

21.

The people of ancient Egypt thought the pharaohs were _____.

22.

What does the word "pharaoh" mean?

23.

Ancient Egyptians thought it was disrespectful to speak directly about the pharaoh so they used the word _____.

24.

To represent both upper and lower Egypt, the pharaoh wore a double _____.

25.

Everyday ruling of Egypt was done by an official who functioned as a prime minister. He was called the _____.

26.

In 1922, a young pharaoh's tomb was discovered. This tomb's contents have toured the world. Who was this young pharaoh?

27.

All houses of Ancient Egypt, from peasants' huts to royal palaces, were built of _____.

28.

The houses of ancient Egypt were built of mudbrick, but if the owner could afford it, the door frame and columns might be made of _____ and _____.

29.

True or false: In ancient Egypt women could not own property.

30.

True or false: Only a royal woman of ancient Egypt could hold public office.

31.

Most large cities of ancient Egypt were built along the Nile River. Why?

32.

Ancient Egypt had three classes of people. The peasants were the lowest class; the nobles were the upper class. Who made up the middle class?

33.

Since paper was so expensive, most writing was done on ostraca. What was ostraca?

34.

In ancient Egypt, things needed for a royal tomb were made by _____.

35.

History shows that builders of royal tombs sometimes went on strike. What fact did they use to pressure the pharaoh to get what they wanted?

36.

On Egyptian tombs, scenes and practical objects were painted. What did the people believe would happen to these objects in the next world?

37.

In stone sculptures, the people of ancient Egypt are always pictured as handsome and young. Why were the sculptures made that way?

38.

In paintings and sculptures where royalty and servants are shown together, the servants are always pictured much smaller than royalty. Why?

39.

You may want to visit the most famous pyramids in Egypt. Where will you go?

40.

Scattered across Egypt today, you can see the ruins of only about how many pyramids?

41.

Why were pyramids built?

42.

Why were pyramids built in the desert and never on the fertile land beside the Nile River?

43.

Pyramids were usually built in groups. The largest one was built for the king. Who was buried in the smaller tombs?

44.

The first capital of Egypt was Memphis. Later the capital was moved to Themes. What is the capital of Egypt today?

45.

In paintings and sculptures of Egyptian gods or goddesses, the head is never pictured as human, but as the head of a _____ or an _____.

46.

An important job in ancient Egypt was to write down everything for the records. The person who did this was called the _____.

47.

The earliest kind of writing used in Egypt was pictured signs. What do we call this writing?

48.

Learning to write in hieroglyphics was a long, hard job. It started at age _____ and lasted until age _____.

49.

The civilization of ancient Egypt ended in 332 B.C. when Egypt was conquered by a famous Greek. Name him.

50.

One of ancient Egypt's most famous rulers was a queen who killed herself when Rome conquered Egypt in 30 B.C. Name this famous queen.

51.

What body of water borders Egypt on the north?

52.

What body of water borders Egypt on the east?

53.

Ancient Egyptians mummified the bodies of the dead. Why?

54.

When preparing the dead, the Egyptians used Canopic jars to preserve what parts of the body?

55.

Houses of all Egyptians, including the royalty, were made of mudbrick. Stone was used to build what buildings?

56.

Outside their temples, ancient Egyptians placed tall pillars cut from a single piece of stone. What is a tall, slender pillar such as this called?

57.

During the Old and Middle Kingdoms of ancient Egypt, the unusual dress for men of all ranks was a _____.

58.

Egyptians mixed ground stone and water to make a green or grey paint for decorating the eyes. What was this mixture called?

59.

Most of what we know of life in ancient Egypt comes from paintings and sculpture found on the walls of _____ and _____.

60.

We know from wall paintings that ancient Egyptians enjoyed music. Name one kind of musical instrument that was used in Egypt.

61.

Ancient Egyptians carried small objects that they thought would keep evil spirits away. Such an object is called an _____.

62.

About 700 B.C., the last and simplest version of hieroglyphics was developed. What was it called?

63.

Ancient Egyptians dried bodies of the dead, covered them with oils and wrapped them in tight bandages. A body prepared in this way is called a _____.

64.

In 1799, a stone discovered in Egypt provided the way to decipher the meaning of Egyptian hieroglyphics. Name this famous stone.

65.

In Egypt, the period from June to September when the Nile flooded was called the _____.

66.

Only one kind of cloth has been found in ancient Egyptian tombs. This cloth was made from flax which grew along the Nile. What kind of cloth is this?

67.

Nearly all tomb paintings of ancient Egypt show everyone dressed in white. How do we know that colored and patterned cloth were also used?

68.

True or false: Because of the heat, most Egyptians liked very short, plain hairstyles.

69.

Men of ancient Egypt wore different kilts depending on their age, job or rank. How were the kilts different?

70.

Royal tombs and temples were often guarded by a sculpture with the head of a man and the body of a lion. This huge sculpture was a _____.

Add these pyramid cards to the regular deck.

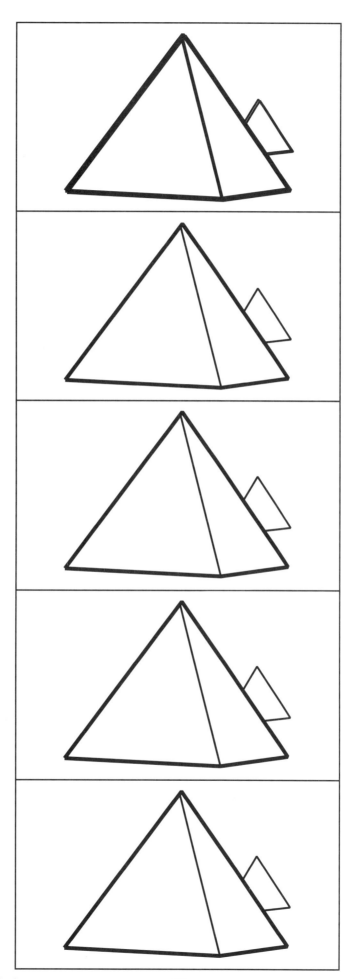

Answer Key for "Climb the Pyramid"

1. Nile River

2. North

3. Mediterranean Sea

4. 3,000 years

5. King Zoser, who died in 2950 B.C.

6. Pharaohs

7. Dynasty

8. Menes

9. Old Kingdom

10. The climate is hot and dry, which prevents items from decaying.

11. They believed possessions went to the next world with the dead.

12. Desert

13. Sun

14. It is the world's longest river, traveling over 4,000 miles.

15. White Nile and Blue Nile

16. True

17. Wheat

18. Papyrus

19. They traded goods and crops.

20. Crops

21. Gods

22. "Great House"

23. Palace

24. Crown

25. Vizier

26. Tutankhamen or King Tut

27. Mudbrick

28. Stone and wood

29. False; women could own property and will it to anyone.

30. True

31. Goods could be easily shipped up and down the river.

32. Artists and craftsmen

33. Broken pieces of pottery

34. Craftsmen

35. It was unthinkable that a pharaoh's tomb would not be finished.

36. The objects would come to life if they were needed.

37. They portrayed how the people wanted to be in the next life.

38. To show that the servants were less important

39. Giza

40. About 30 (about 60 more are in Sudan, south of Egypt)

41. They were built as tombs for the body and possessions of royalty.

42. All the fertile land was needed for growing food.

43. The queen and other favored wives

44. Cairo

45. Bird or animal

46. Scribe

47. Hieroglyphics

48. Age 4 to age 16

49. Alexander the Great

50. Cleopatra VII

51. Mediterranean Sea

52. Red Sea

53. To preserve them for life in the next world

54. Internal organs and the brain.

55. Temples of gods and goddesses

56. Obelisk

57. Kilt

58. Kohl

59. Temples and tombs

60. Harp, lute, or pipe

61. Amulet

62. Demotic

63. Mummy

64. Rosetta Stone

65. Inundation

66. Linen

67. Brightly colored garments were found in King Tut's tomb.

68. False; Egyptians liked long, elaborate hairstyles.

69. In length; kilts came to the knee, calf, or ankle

70. Sphinx

It's All Greek to Me

This game reviews the students' knowledge about Greece. The game can be played with the entire class or the class can be divided into groups, with each group receiving its own stack of cards, rules, and answer key. Add several "It's All Greek to Me" cards to each stack. If there is more time after a round of play, have groups exchange cards to play again.

Purpose: to review knowledge about ancient Greece

Materials Needed:

- card stock of any color to print game cards, rules and answer key
- laminating materials

Construction:

1. Print pages with game cards on colored card stock. Laminate pages, then cut cards apart.
2. Trim rules and answer key boxes. Print on card stock of same color as used for game cards. Laminate them.

Rules for "It's All Greek to Me"

This game is for three to four players and one judge.

1. Judge shuffles cards, including the 10 cards that say "It's All Greek to Me," and places them on table, word side down.

2. Player to judge's left goes first. Play moves to the left.

3. First player takes a card and reads number and question aloud. Player attempts to answer the question. Judge checks the answer key.

4. Judge scores as follows:

   Correct answer: Keep the card. Next player's turn.

   Incorrect answer: Card is shuffled back into the card pile to be used again.

6. If players gets a card that says "It's All Greek to Me," player keeps that card, takes one card from any other player, and takes another turn.

7. Player who ends up with the most cards is the winner. Count any "It's All Greek to Me" cards as part of final score.

1.

The ancient Greeks left a legacy of learning and ideas for later civilizations to build on. What is a legacy?

2.

Greece is located in the southern part of what continent?

3.

The earliest known civilizations of Greece were on an island in the Mediterranean Sea. Name this island.

4.

The first important civilization of Greece began on the island of Crete. Name this civilization.

5.

Greece has two land areas that are connected by the Isthmus of Corinth. What is an isthmus?

6.

The southern part of Greece is a large peninsula. What is a peninsula?

7.

The southern peninsula of early Greece was called _____.

8.

Name the two most famous cities of early Greece.

9.

What sea borders Greece on the east?

10.

What sea borders Greece on the west?

11.

What city of ancient Greece was the site of the first Olympic games?

12.

A famous hero of Greek literature made his home on the Greek island of Ithaca. Name this hero.

13.

Name the general of early Greece who led Athens through the Golden Age.

14.

Most of our knowledge of Greece has come from the Classical Age, which lasted 100 years. We usually call this time the _____ Age of Greece.

15.

Mountains of Greece were natural boundaries which divided early Greece into many small _____ which ruled themselves.

16.

True or False: Although separated into many city-states, the people of early Greece all spoke the same language.

17.

The mountains of Greece were not very high except for one, which stood at nearly 10 thousand feet. Name this mountain.

18.

From any spot in Greece, you can reach the sea by traveling about how many miles?

19.

What type of government was ancient Greece's gift to the world?

20.

The word democracy comes from two Greek words, demos and kratos. Kratos means "to rule." What does demos means?

21.

Because of the many small islands surrounding the mainland of Greece, two occupations became more important than any others. Name these two occupations.

22.

If you sailed west through the Strait of Gibraltar and continued across the sea to Greece, what sea would you be crossing?

23.

Most Greek city-states were built around a high fortress called the _____.

24.

The ruins of a famous acropolis can be seen in the modern-day city of _____.

25.

The Minoan civilization on the island of Crete lasted 1,500 years. This civilization was named for what king?

26.

Scientists called _____ learn about ancient Greece by digging up and studying cities and artifacts.

27.

The Cretans of the Minoan civilization learned to make _____ by heating and mixing tin and copper.

28.

To protect their merchant ships and shoreline from pirates, the Minoans formed the world's first _____.

29.

The entrance to the oldest city on the mainland of Greece is still guarded today by two carved lions. Name this city.

30.

When royalty of Mycenae died, they were placed in large, ornate tombs. Why were such large, ornate tombs used?

31.

A famous king of Mycenae was Agamemnon. He led the Greeks to victory in their famous battle with the city of _____.

32.

Troy was located on the eastern side of the Aegean Sea in what is now the country of _____.

33.

A love affair between Paris of Troy and Helen, the wife of the King of Sparta, started a war that lasted 10 years. Name this war.

34.

The Greeks won the Trojan War because they hid soldiers in the famous _____ _____, which they left at the gate of the city of Troy.

35.

Zeus was the king of the Greek gods. Name the Greek god of the underworld.

36.

After the wonderful civilizations of Minoa and Troy disappeared, Greece went through a long period known as the _____ _____.

37.

During the Dark Age of Greece, tribes ruled themselves in groups. These groups came to be called _____.

38.

The center of the city-state was an open space that was a meeting place and market. What was this place called?

39.

Some city-states formed governments that were called oligarchies. What is an oligarchy?

40.

Some city-states became democracies. What is a democracy?

41.

Some city-states were taken over by tyrants. What is a tyrant?

42.

True or False: Most city-states of Middle Age Greece were small, with populations of 5,000–10,000 people.

43.

Name the Greek city-state that had the largest population (about 40,000).

44.

It took about two days to walk across the largest city-state. Name this city-state.

45.

During the Golden Age, the two strongest city-states were _____ and _____.

46.

Name the city-state that was a strict military state where physical fitness and a well-trained army were most important.

47.

Which city-state had a strong navy and was a center of the arts?

48.

In 432 B.C., Athens and her allies fought a war with Sparta and her allies. What was this war called?

49.

The Peloponnesian War lasted for 27 years. Who finally won this war?

50.

True or False: The downfall of Greece was caused because the city-states were never willing to unite.

51.

By 238 B.C., one man had gained control of all of Greece by conquering the city-states one by one. Name this man.

52.

The son of Philip of Macedonia followed his father in ruling Greece. He conquered the known world of his time. Name this famous conqueror.

53.

After the death of Alexander the Great, Greece fell under the control of the _____ Empire.

54.

Name the famous Greek teacher who was a tutor for Alexander the Great.

55.

True or False: Women were allowed to vote in Ancient Greece.

56.

True or False: Since education was so important in early Greece, girls received the same fine education as boys did.

57.

History tells us that about one-third of the total population of early Greece were _____.

58.

True or False: Because of the warm, sunny climate, most activity of Greek life took place outside.

59.

Greeks usually knocked on the door of their homes as they went out. Why?

60.

A common food of early Greece was a pancake-like bread made from wheat or barley. What was this bread called?

61.

True or False: In Ancient Greece, meat was plentiful and all people ate it often.

62.

Name three beverages that might be served at a Greek meal.

63.

True or False: Early Greeks did not use silverware to eat.

64.

The main item of Greek clothing was a piece of cloth pinned and tied to make a tunic called a _____.

65.

True or False: Greek clothing had no pockets so Greeks carried money tucked in their mouths.

66.

On cool evenings, early Greeks wore an outer wrap over the tunic. What was this outer wrap called?

67.

True or False: Jewelry was not known to the Early Greeks.

68.

The most important work of the men of Sparta was to be prepared for _____.

69.

What was the major occupation of the people of Athens?

70.

Why was raising sheep so important in Athens?

71.

Which city-state was ruled by two kings, a council of citizens, and five overseers called ephors?

72.

The overseers of Sparta were elected each year and were very powerful. What were these overseers called?

73.

True or False: In Sparta, babies that were not born strong and healthy were left on a mountain to die of exposure.

74.

Which Greek city-state founded the first democracy in the history of the world?

75.

In Athens, laws were voted on and officials were elected by a body of men called the _____.

76.

If you were meeting with the Council of 500 to discuss problems of the citizens, what city-state would you be in?

77.

Name the city-state where 10% of all the people were soldiers.

78.

Most people of Sparta fell into the lowest social class—just above slaves. What was this group called?

79.

To be a citizen in Athens, a man's parents had to be born in Athens and he had to be _____ years old.

80.

About half of the people of Athens were in a group that could do any job they wanted, but they could not own farms or vote. What was this group called?

81.

True or False: There were no slaves in Athens.

82.

At what age did a boy of Sparta leave his home to begin his military training?

83.

What was the job of all Spartan men from age 18 to age 30?

84.

The law in Sparta said that men must stay in the army until age 30 and then they must _____.

85.

Name the ruler of Athens who first allowed citizens to make their own laws through an Assembly.

86.

Heavy, slow merchant ships of Greece were protected by light, fast warships called _____.

87.

The law of Athens said that all 18-year-old men must join the army for how many years?

88.

Modern Olympic Games began as a religious festival held every four years to honor which Greek god?

89.

The main event of early Olympic Games included five different sports. What was this event called?

90.

Name the five sports included in the pentathlon of Greek Olympic games.

91.

Name the Greek poet who wrote *The Iliad* and *The Odyssey.*

92.

The long poem, *The Illiad*, describes what famous Greek war?

93.

What famous Greek poem describes the adventures of Odysseus on his way home from the Trojan War?

94.

Name the Greek goddess of wisdom.

95.

What are the first and last letters of the Greek alphabet?

96.

Name the three greatest Greek philosophers.

97.

The water passage connecting the Mediterranean Sea and the Atlantic Ocean is called the Strait of Gibraltar. Early Greeks had another name for this strait. What was this name?

98.

If you rented a house in Athens and did not pay the rent, what might the landlord do?

99.

The _____ was a temple built in Athens to honor the goddess Athena.

100.

The writer of such famous fables as "The Hare and the Tortoise" and "The Fox and the Grapes" lived in ancient Greece. His fables always ended with a moral. Name this famous writer of fables.

It's All Greek To Me

It's All Greek To Me

It's All Greek To Me

It's All Greek To Me

It's All Greek To Me

It's All Greek To Me

It's All Greek To Me

It's All Greek To Me

It's All Greek To Me

It's All Greek To Me

Answer Key for "It's All Greek to Me"

1. A gift from the past

2. Europe

3. Crete

4. Minoan Civilization

5. A narrow strip of land that connects two larger areas of land

6. A body of land that is almost entirely surrounded by water

7. Peloponnesus

8. Sparta and Athens

9. Aegean Sea

10. Ionian Sea

11. Olympia

12. Odysseus

13. Pericles

14. Golden

15. Cities or city-states

16. True

17. Mount Olympus

18. Fifty

19. Democracy

20. "The people"

21. Trade and fishing

22. Mediterranean Sea

23. Acropolis

24. Athens

25. King Minos

26. Archaeologists

27. Bronze

28. Navy

29. Mycenae

30. They believed the tombs would be homes in the afterlife.

31. Troy

32. Turkey

33. Trojan War

34. Trojan Horse

35. Hades

36. Dark Ages or Middle Ages

37. City-states

38. The agora

39. Government by a few select people

40. Government by the people

41. A ruler who has complete control

42. True

43. Athens

44. Attica

45. Sparta and Athens

46. Sparta

47. Athens

48. Peloponnesian War

49. Sparta

50. True

51. Philip of Macedonia

52. Alexander the Great

53. Roman

54. Aristotle

55. False

56. False

57. Slaves

58. True

59. The streets were very narrow and a passerby might be hit by the door.

60. Artes

61. False; only the wealthy ate meat very often

62. Water, goat's milk, wine

63. True

64. Chiton

65. True

66. Himation

67. False; both men and women wore jewelry.

68. War or battle

69. Farming

70. Sheep were used for meat, milk, and wool.

71. Sparta

72. Ephors

73. True

74. Athens

75. Assembly or Ecclesia

76. Athens

77. Sparta

78. Helots

79. 18

80. Metics

81. False; slaves did most of the work.

82. Seven

83. To fight in the army

84. Marry and raise strong children

85. Solon

86. Tiremes

87. Two

88. Zeus

89. Pentathlon

90. Foot race, discus throw, long jump, wrestling, and javelin throw

91. Homer

92. Trojan War

93. *The Odyssey*

94. Athena

95. Alpha and Omega

96. Socrates, Plato, and Aristotle

97. Gates of Hercules

98. Remove the front door, remove roof tiles, and stop up the well

99. Parthenon

100. Aesop

Konnichiwa, Nihon (Hello, Japan)

Here are 50 questions to help players say *konnichiwa* (koe-nee-chee-wah) to Japan. Konnichiwa is a greeting that means "good morning," "good day," or "hello."

Purpose: to practice and review knowledge of Japan

Material Needed:

- white card stock to print game cards and to mount rules and answer key boxes
- red marker
- laminating materials

Construction:

1. Print the game card pages on white card stock. Laminate the pages and cut the cards apart.

2. Page 113 has cards with a circle in their center. Copy this page onto card stock and color the circles red to make Japanese flags. Laminate the colored flags page and cut the cards apart.

3. Trim the rules and answer key boxes. Mount on white card stock. Laminate them.

Rules for "Konnichiwa, Nihon (Hello, Japan)"

This game is for three to four players and one judge.

1. Judge shuffles all cards, including the five flag cards, and places the cards face down.

2. Player to judge's left goes first. Play moves to the left.

3. First player takes a card and reads the card number and question aloud. Player attempts to answer the question. The judge will tell the player if the answer is correct.

4. If the card drawn shows the Japanese flag, the player keeps that card, takes one card from any other player, and takes another turn.

5. Players earn points by keeping cards for questions they have answered correctly. When a player incorrectly answers a question, the card is shuffled back into the card pile to be used again.

6. Play ends when all cards have been used or when game time is over. Player having the most cards is the winner. Count any flag cards as part of the final score.

1.

Japan is a horseshoe-shaped island chain that is a part of what continent?

2.

Japan is separated from the mainland of Asia by what sea?

3.

Japan's capital city is also the largest city in the country. Name this city.

4.

On which of Japan's islands is the capital city located?

5.

What ocean borders Japan on the east?

6.

What percent of Japan's land is made up of high mountains and hills?

7.

Japan is made up of over 3,600 islands. The four main islands are Kyushu, Shikoku, Hokkaido, and the largest island which is named _____.

8.

Japan's land area in square miles is about the same as what U.S. state?

9.

What is the name of Japan's highest mountain? On which island is this mountain located?

10.

At its widest point, Japan is about how many miles wide?

11.

The Japanese language takes many years to learn because it has 2,000 _____ and two _____.

12.

Although younger Japanese have adopted western ways, many older Japanese cling to traditional ways. What does traditional mean?

13.

Japan has more large cities than any other country except one. Name this country.

14.

What is Japan's monetary unit?

15.

The second largest city in Japan is only 30 minutes away from Tokyo. Name this city.

16.

True or False: There is very little crime in Japan.

17.

Just as school students in America have regular fire drills, Japanese schools have regular drills for what disaster?

18.

Many Japanese still use the traditional way of greeting others; instead of shaking hands, they _____.

19.

The Japanese have not adopted the western habit of eating. They still eat with _____.

20.

When eating with Japanese friends, it is good manners to wait to start until which person in the group has started?

21.

Japan's most important food is eaten in most families for breakfast, lunch, and dinner. What is this food?

22.

At a Japanese meal, it is polite to eat every grain of rice from your bowl. If you leave any rice, it may be taken as a sign that you _____.

23.

Sashimi is one of the most famous foods in Japan. What is sashimi?

24.

If you are giving someone in Japan a gift, it is best to give items in odd lots such as three, five, or seven. Items given in even lots would be considered _____.

25.

Many Japanese people enjoy the art of beautiful handwriting known as _____.

26.

In the U.S. everyone who is 18 and older may vote. In Japan, you must be how old to vote?

27.

The emperor of Japan is only a symbolic head of state and has no real power. What official is the actual head of the government?

28.

At what age do Japanese children start school?

29.

At age 12, all Japanese students begin to learn what language?

30.

What is the name of Japan's most famous shopping street?

31.

The floors of Japanese homes do not have carpets, but are covered with thick mats. The straw in these mats comes from what kind of grain?

32.

What is Japan's national sport?

33.

What is the most popular sport in Japan?

34.

In Japan, there is a large Disneyland where visitors are greeted in Japanese by _____.

35.

Japanese specialize in the art of growing miniature trees. This is done by continual pruning of the roots and branches. What are these miniature trees called?

36.

Japan has one of the world's fastest trains. It travels at speeds up to 155 miles per hour. What is this train called?

37.

The traditional costume of Japan is a loose robe with wide sleeves. What is this robe called?

38.

Ancient warriors of Japan were known as _____.

39.

The Japanese have more festivals than any other country in the world. Name Japan's most important festival.

40.

Autumn in Japan is the typhoon season. What is a typhoon?

41. 🏯

Before entering the house, people in Japan take off their _____.

42. 🏯

Many Japanese people spread thin mattresses on the floor for sleeping. What are these mattresses called?

43. 🏯

Name the two main religions practiced by the Japanese people.

44. 🏯

On May 5, Japanese families with sons celebrate by flying huge kites that are shaped like brightly colored paper fish. What holiday is this?

45. 🏯

On March 3, Japanese families with daughters set up a display of beautiful dolls on a red velvet stand. What is this holiday?

46. 🏯

In 1941, the U.S. went to war with Japan after Japan attacked the U.S. Naval Base in Hawaii. Name this Naval Base.

47. 🏯

In 1945, World War II ended. Japan surrendered after the U.S. dropped atomic bombs on the cities of _____ and _____.

48. 🏯

Japan enjoys three kinds of theater. One is Noh, a drama in which all the actors wear _____.

49. 🏯

One kind of Japanese drama is Kabuki which takes place on a huge revolving stage and where all the parts are played by _____.

50. 🏯

Bunraku is a form of Japanese drama in which solemn tragedies are acted out by life-like _____.

Color the circles red.

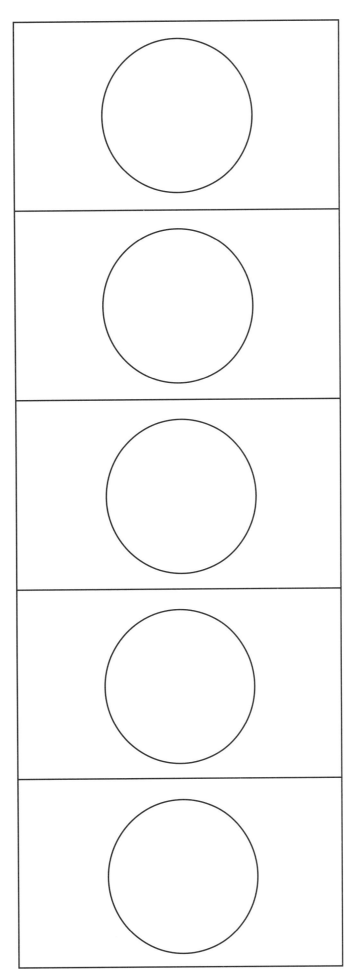

Answer Key for "Konnichiwa, Nihon"

1. Asia
2. Sea of Japan
3. Tokyo
4. Honshu
5. Pacific Ocean
6. Over 70%
7. Honshu
8. Montana
9. Mount Fuji; Honshu
10. 250
11. Characters; alphabets
12. Not modern; doing things the old way
13. United States
14. The yen
15. Yokohama
16. True
17. Earthquake
18. Bow
19. Chopsticks
20. The oldest person at the table
21. Rice
22. Want more
23. Raw fish
24. Bad luck
25. Calligraphy
26. Age 20
27. Prime Minister
28. Age 5
29. English
30. The Ginza
31. Rice
32. Sumo wrestling
33. Baseball
34. Mickey Mouse
35. Bonsai
36. Bullet Train
37. Kimono
38. Samurai
39. The New Year Festival
40. A hurricane-like storm with strong winds and rain
41. Shoes
42. Futons
43. Buddhism; Shinto
44. Children's Day
45. Girl's Festival
46. Pearl Harbor
47. Hiroshima; Nagasaki
48. Masks
49. Men
50. Puppets

The Shamrock Patch

Two groups can play this game about Ireland at the same time. Divide the 70 question cards into two equal stacks and place 10 of the penalty/reward cards into each stack. Decorate the back of each game card with a shamrock sticker and lay the cards out in a grid pattern of nine cards across and five cards down to create a "shamrock patch." To answer a question, a player must pick a shamrock from the shamrock patch.

Purpose: to practice and review knowledge about Ireland

Materials Needed:

- light green card stock to print game cards and mount rules and answer key
- small shamrock stickers to decorate backs of the game cards
- laminating material

Construction:

1. Print the game card pages onto green card stock.

2. Trim the rules and answer key boxes. Mount on card stock of the same color as used for the game cards. Decorate with shamrock stickers. Laminate them.

 Rules for "The Shamrock Patch"

This game is for three or four players and one judge.

1. Judge shuffles all cards and arranges them in a 5 x 9 grid with shamrock side up.
2. Player to judge's left goes first. Player moves to the left.
3. First player picks any card and reads the number of the card and the question aloud. Player attempts to answer the question. The judge will tell the player if he or she is correct, but will not read the correct answer if the player is incorrect.
4. Judge scores as follows:
   Correct answer: Player keeps the card. Next player's turn.
   Incorrect answer: Return the card to the spot from which it came for another player to pick up.
5. When a player picks a penalty or reward card, he or she must follow its instruction.
6. When all the shamrock cards have been picked or when game time is over, each player counts their cards. Player with the most cards wins.

1.

Ireland is a large island located in the northern part of what ocean?

2.

The island of Ireland is divided into two parts. Name them.

3.

The Republic of Ireland is independently governed, but North Ireland is a part of the country of _____.

4.

The capital and largest city of the Republic of Ireland is _____.

5.

Because of its beautiful color, Ireland is sometimes called "The _____ Isle"

6.

Ireland is often called the land of the _____ because these animals are shipped from Ireland to all parts of the world.

7.

One-tenth of Ireland is swampy land called _____.

8.

One of Ireland's most important resources is used for both heating and cooking. What is this resource?

9.

What is another name for peat?

10.

Name the sea that separates Ireland from Great Britain.

11. 🍀

"Lough" (pronounced lahk) is the Irish word for _____.

12. 🍀

Name Ireland's largest lake.

13. 🍀

Name Ireland's longest river.

14. 🍀

Name two of Ireland's four provinces.

15. 🍀

Does Northern Ireland or the Republic of Ireland occupy most of the island of Ireland?

16. 🍀

Like young Americans, young people in Dublin, Ireland eat _____ and go to the movies.

17. 🍀

Name the city that is the capital and chief port of Northern Ireland.

18. 🍀

What is the native language of Ireland?

19. 🍀

Many Irish names begin with "Mac" (as in Macmillan) or "O" (as in O'Brien). What is the meaning of each of these prefixes?

20. 🍀

What language do most Irish people speak?

21.

Name the Irish author who wrote *Gulliver's Travels.*

22.

Oliver Goldsmith was an early Irish writer who first compiled a book of children's _____ _____.

23.

Name the most famous of Irish saints.

24.

On what day do we celebrate St. Patrick's Day?

25.

Name two fabrics for which the Irish are famous.

26.

According to Irish folklore, mischievous elves can bring bad luck. What are these impish elves called?

27.

One leprechaun of Irish folklore is a rich fairy who is banker for all fairies. He keeps the fairies' gold in a pot which he keeps at the _____.

28.

Name an Irish sport that is played with broad, flat sticks and a small leather ball.

29.

Hurling is an Irish game that is most like what American game?

30.

Gaelic football uses a round ball and is like both American football and what other popular sport?

31.

The "sport of kings" is popular in Ireland. What sport is the "sport of kings?"

32.

What sport is popular in Ireland because of the many lakes and rivers?

33.

Ireland's highest mountains are in what national park?

34.

What transportation restriction is there in Ireland's Muckross National Park?

35.

Galway is a well-known county of Ireland. The people of Galway say that a famous explorer stopped there on his way to the New World. Name this explorer.

36.

The first Irish people who came to America settled in which two colonies?

37.

Many Irish fought in the 1700s in what famous American war?

38.

John Barry, an Irish navy man, was captain of the first American fighting ship. By what title does history know John Barry?

39.

In 1776, four men of Irish birth were among the 56 signers of a very famous document of our country. Name this document.

40.

Charles Thomson from Derry County, Ireland, designed one of our American symbols. Name this symbol.

41.

An Irish architect designed the White House in Washington, D.C. Name this architect.

42.

James Hoban, an Irish architect, designed the original White House in the 1700s. In the 1980s, the U.S. honored James Hoban in what way?

43.

The great grandfather of one U.S. President came to America in 1850 to escape Ireland's Great Potato Famine. Name the president.

44.

A famous Irish writer is known for classics such as *The Dubliners* and *Ulysses.* Name this famous writer.

45.

A son of an Irish immigrant developed the "Model T" and started a well-known American automobile company. Name him.

46.

John MacDonald, the son of Irish immigrants, was in charge of building the subway system in what large U.S. city?

47.

Louis Henry Sullivan, the son of a wandering Irish musician, designed the first modern American building known as a _____.

48.

Ireland's motto is "Erin Go Bragh." What is the English meaning of this motto?

49.

What plant became a religious symbol in Ireland because St. Patrick used it to explain some of his teachings?

50.

The first St. Patrick's Day parade was held in the U.S. in 1779 in what city?

51.

Besides St. Patrick's Day, another spring holiday had its start in old Irish custom. Name this "tricky" day.

52.

Irish children do not have Easter baskets, but they do decorate eggs. What contest do they have with these eggs?

53.

A terrible time in Irish history was the Great Potato Famine. What is a famine?

54.

An Old Gaelic saying often displayed in Irish homes and inns is "cead mile failte." What is the English translation of this saying?

55.

What is the answer to this Irish riddle:
It's round as an apple,
As deep as a cup
And all the men in Ireland
Could not lift it up.

56.

What does this Irish saying mean: "A word is more lasting than the wealth of the world"?

57.

Irish tradition says that a bride will have good luck if she will wear four different things at her wedding. What are they?

58.

If an Irish friend said to you, "I will see you 'this day week,'" when would you expect to see your friend again?

59.

Many Irish terms are very different from American terms. We go into a food shop and ask for a "soft drink" or a "soda pop." The Irish would ask for a "_____."

60.

Instead of "line up," Irish people say "_____."

61.

A little over half of Ireland's people live in urban areas. What does urban mean?

62.

About 99% of Ireland's people are literate. What does literate mean?

63.

All children in Ireland are required by law to attend school from age _____ to age _____.

64.

The oldest college in Ireland is Trinity College which is also known as the University of _____, the city where it is located.

65.

Ireland's U2 gives performances all over the world. What is U2?

66.

About 70% of Ireland is what kind of land?

67.

Tourism is important to Ireland. Many people from the U.S. visit Ireland each year to find out about their genealogy. What is genealogy?

68.

What is Ireland's national airline called?

69.

In 1970, Irish miners discovered that some of Europe's largest supplies of two important minerals are in eastern Ireland. Name these two minerals.

70.

The government of Ireland has a president, a prime minister, and a _____, which makes the laws.

Green is your favorite color. You must be Irish! Keep this card and take one card from any player.

Isn't this a grand day? Keep this card and take one card from any player.

You are "as busy as a bee." Keep this card and take one card from any player.

You found a four-leaf clover. Keep this card and take one card from any player.

You lost your way and cannot find the pot of gold. Give this card to the player on your left.

"This weather is enough to knock the top off your head." Give this card to the player on your right.

You "counted your chickens before they hatched." Give this card to any player you choose.

Keep this card, but lose your next turn while you visit the "sweet shop" to buy candy.

You forgot to wear green on St. Patrick's Day. Give away this card and another card to the player on your right.

Your car broke down. You must look under the "bonnet" to find the trouble and get the tools out of the "boot" to fix the car. Keep this card, but lose your turn while you fix your car.

You misspelled "leprechaun" on the weekly spelling test. Give this card to the player on your left.

You found a four-leaf clover. Keep this card and take another turn.

You made a foul while playing the Irish game of hurling. Give this card to any player you choose.

You have learned to speak Gaelic. Good for you! Keep this card and take another turn.

While visiting in Muckross National Park, you picked the wildflowers, which is not allowed. Keep this card, but lose your next turn.

You read *Gulliver's Travels* for your book report. Keep this card and take one card from any player you choose.

Your birthday is on the same day as St. Patrick's Day. Keep this card and take another turn.

You don't like potatoes. Give this card and one other card to the player on your right.

Your family is taking a vacation to visit Ireland and trace your family tree. Keep this card and take another turn.

You did an excellent job on the map of Ireland that you had to make for social studies class. Keep this card and take another turn.

Answer Key for "The Shamrock Patch"

1. Atlantic Ocean
2. Northern Ireland; Republic of Ireland
3. Great Britain
4. Dublin
5. Emerald
6. Horse
7. Peat bogs
8. Peat
9. Turf
10. Irish Sea
11. Lake
12. Lough Neagh
13. Shannon River
14. Munster; Leinster; Connacht; Ulster
15. Republic of Ireland
16. hamburgers
17. Belfast
18. Gaelic
19. "Mac" means "son of"
    "O" means "grandson of"
20. English
21. Jonathan Swift
22. Nursery Rhymes
23. St. Patrick
24. March 17
25. Linen and tweed
26. Leprechauns
27. End of the rainbow
28. Hurling
29. Hockey
30. Soccer
31. Horse racing
32. Fishing
33. Muckross National Park
34. No cars are allowed
35. Christopher Columbus
36. Maryland and Pennsylvania
37. American Revolution
38. Father of the American Navy
39. Declaration of Independence
40. Great Seal of the United States
41. James Hoban
42. Postage stamp issued in his honor
43. President John F. Kennedy
44. James Joyce
45. Henry Ford
46. New York
47. Skyscraper
48. "Ireland Forever"
49. Shamrock
50. New York City
51. April Fool's Day
52. They see who can eat the most eggs.
53. Dry time when nothing grows; people starve
54. A hundred thousand welcomes
55. A well
56. Your word means more than your wealth
57. Something old, something new, something borrowed, something blue
58. A week from today
59. Mineral
60. Queue up
61. City
62. Able to read and write
63. Six, 15
64. Dublin
65. A rock music group
66. Farmland or pastureland
67. A person's family ancestry
68. Aer Lingus
69. Lead and zinc
70. Parliament

Down Mexico Way

This game can be played in two or three groups or as a review activity for the entire class. Be sure to add the "Buenos días, amigo" cards to the deck.

Purpose: to review knowledge about a North American neighbor

Materials Needed:

- card stock of any color to print game cards and to mount rules and answer key
- laminating materials

Construction:

1. Print the game card pages on colored card stock. Laminate the pages, then cut cards apart.
2. Trim the rules and answer key boxes. Mount on card stock of the same color as used for game cards. Laminate them.

Rules for "Down Mexico Way"

This game is for three or four players and one judge.

1. Judge shuffles the cards, including the ten cards that say "Buenos días, amigo." Spread cards face down.

2. Player to judge's left goes first. Play moves to the left.

3. First player: Take a card and read card number and question aloud. Attempt to answer the question. The judge tells if the answer is correct.

4. Players earn points by keeping cards for questions they have answered correctly. When a player incorrectly answers a question, the judge reads the correct answer and the card is shuffled back into the card pile to be used again.

5. If a player gets a card that says "Buenos días, amigo," he or she keeps that card, takes one card from any player, and takes another turn.

6. Play is over when all cards have been used or when game time is over. Player having the most cards is the winner.

1.

Mexico is part of what continent?

2.

Mexico is a blend of what two cultures?

3.

In 1993, the North American Free Trade Agreement (NAFTA) was signed by three countries to create a common market. Name these three countries.

4.

Southeast Mexico has a large peninsula that extends northwest into the Gulf of Mexico. Name this peninsula.

5.

Mexico is bordered on the east by what body of water?

6.

The most northwestern part of Mexico is a long, narrow peninsula. Name this peninsula.

7.

What body of water separates Baja California from the mainland of Mexico?

8.

Name the four states of the United States that border Mexico on its north.

9.

What river forms the border between Texas and Mexico?

10.

What body of water borders Mexico on the west?

11.

What sea borders the Yucatan Peninsula on the east?

12.

Two great mountain chains run the length of Mexico. Name them.

13.

When Spaniards reached Mexico in 1519, they found a powerful Indian tribe there. Name this Indian tribe.

14.

In the early 1500s, the Spaniards defeated the Indians and gained control of what is now Mexico. They named their new colony _____.

15.

Nearly 80% of the population of Mexico is of mixed native and Spanish ancestry. People with this heritage are called _____.

16.

There are over 50 different native languages spoken in Mexico, but the official language of the country is _____.

17.

The capital of Mexico is the fourth largest city in Mexico with over 15 million people. Name this capital city.

18.

The capital of Mexico is the world's fourth largest city in population. Which world city has the largest population?

19.

The U.S. is divided into 50 states; Canada has 10 provinces. What are the divisions of Mexico called and how many are there?

20.

Mexico has four cities that have over a million in population. Name these four cities.

21.

What two Latin American countries border Mexico on the south?

22.

The Rio Grande River separates Mexico and Texas. The people of Mexico do not call this river the Rio Grande. What do they call it?

23.

Mexico has the third largest mountain peak in North America. It is an extinct snow-capped volcano located southeast of Mexico City. Name this peak.

24.

This most important basic food of Mexico is used in making tortillas. Name this food.

25.

A Mexican stew food that is popular in the U.S. is made with beef, beans, tomatoes, and spices. Name this food.

26.

Bullfighting and baseball are popular in Mexico, but the most popular spectator sport is _____.

27.

The people of Mexico like a handball game in which players use long wicker baskets. Name this game.

28.

In what month do the people of Mexico celebrate Labor Day?

29.

Mexico's Independence Day is celebrated on what date?

30.

By far, the most popular and elaborate religious celebration of the year in Mexico is _____.

31.

What is the Spanish word for celebration or festival?

32.

A popular Mexican event is the *charreadas*, a display of horsemanship skills, somewhat like the _____ in the United States.

33.

What is the Spanish word for cowboys?

34.

True or False: Few Mexican homes have television sets.

35.

Almost 90% of the people of Mexico follow what religion?

36.

At Christmas, children of Mexico enjoy swinging at and breaking open a hanging container that is filled with toys and candy. What is this container called?

37.

Book publishing is an important industry in Mexico. In fact, the first _____ in the New World was used in Mexico in 1539.

38.

In the U.S., the basic unit of money is the dollar; in Mexico the basic unit of money is the _____.

39.

True or False: Most people of Mexico own an automobile.

40.

Give two reasons why only about 50% of Mexico's land is suitable for farming and grazing.

41.

Mexico is the world's fifth largest producer of _____, which is vital to transportation.

42.

Mexico leads the world in the production of what precious metal?

43.

What country is Mexico's most important trading partner?

44.

What is the second largest source of income in Mexico?

45.

One of Mexico's most famous and most popular resorts is located on the southwest coast. Name it.

46.

Running the length of Mexico is the _____ Highway which links the U.S. with 17 Latin American countries.

47.

Mexico's leading seaport is located on the Gulf of Mexico. Name this port.

48.

In Mexico, education is free and required by law for all children between the ages of _____ and _____.

49.

In September, Mexico celebrates Independence Day just as we do in July. In 1821, Mexico gained independence from what European country?

50.

In 1836, U.S. settlers living north of the Rio Grande River revolted against Mexican rule and established the Republic of _____.

51.

As a result of a war with Mexico in 1846–1847, the U.S. gained from Mexico all or part of what four present-day states?

52.

The most famous battle of the 1846–1847 war between the U.S. and Mexico took place at a popular present-day tourist site in San Antonio, Texas. Name this site.

53.

The land gained by the U.S. from Mexico during and after the Mexican War was what percent of the total land area of Mexico?

54.

Rodolfo Neri became the first Mexican to join a U.S. crew in 1985 to do what?

55.

The three largest states of Mexico are along the southwest border of the U.S. Name these three Mexican states.

56.

Mexico's official name is Estados Unidos Mexicanos. What does this mean in English?

57.

Mexico's flag has three vertical stripes, with the coat of arms in the center stripe. What are the colors of the three stripes?

58.

The head of the U.S. government is a president. What official heads the government of Mexico?

59.

Like the United States, Mexico's government has three branches. Name these three branches.

60.

The U.S. president serves one term of four years. How long is one term for the president of Mexico?

61.

How do you say "Merry Christmas" in Spanish?

62.

A popular Christmas celebration in Mexico is the nine days of parades to re-enact the journey of Mary and Joseph to Bethlehem. What is this nine-day trial called?

63.

What does the Spanish word *posada* mean in English?

64.

True or False: Most of Mexico's people live in rural areas.

65.

Count 1–10 in Spanish.

66.

Mexico's largest lake, in the state of Jalisco, is 53 miles long and 16 miles wide. Name this lake.

67.

In small villages and rural areas, buying and selling often takes place in a *tiangui*. What is a *tiangui*?

68.

A major issue between the U.S. and Mexico has been immigration. How does someone become a legal immigrant?

69.

Because of the heat in Mexico, most shops and offices close for a long lunch hour during which many people have a *siesta*. What is a *siesta*?

70.

You are leaving Mexico after a wonderful visit. How will you say "Goodbye, friend" in Spanish?

BUENOS DÍAS, AMIGO

BUENOS DÍAS, AMIGO

BUENOS DÍAS, AMIGO

BUENOS DÍAS, AMIGO

BUENOS DÍAS, AMIGO

BUENOS DÍAS, AMIGO

BUENOS DÍAS, AMIGO

BUENOS DÍAS, AMIGO

BUENOS DÍAS, AMIGO

BUENOS DÍAS, AMIGO

Answer Key for "Down Mexico Way"

1. North America
2. Spanish and Native Mexican
3. Canada, U.S., Mexico
4. Yucatan Peninsula
5. Gulf of Mexico
6. Baja California
7. Gulf of California
8. California, Arizona, New Mexico, Texas
9. Rio Grande River
10. Pacific Ocean
11. Caribbean Sea
12. Sierra Madre Occidental and Sierra Madre Oriental
13. Aztecs
14. New Spain
15. Mestizos
16. Spanish
17. Mexico City
18. Tokyo
19. States; 31
20. Guadalajara, Monterrey, Pueblo, Mexico City
21. Guatemala, Belize
22. Rio Bravo
23. Mt. Orizaba (Citlaltepetl)
24. Corn
25. Chili con carne
26. Soccer
27. Jai alai
28. May
29. September 16
30. Christmas
31. Fiesta
32. Rodeo
33. Charros
34. False: 70% have TV
35. Catholic
36. Piñata
37. Printing press
38. Peso
39. False: less than 30% own cars
40. Dry climate; high mountains
41. Oil
42. Silver
43. United States
44. Tourism
45. Acapulco
46. Pan American
47. Veracruz
48. 6, 16
49. Spain
50. Texas
51. New Mexico, Texas, California, and Arizona
52. The Alamo
53. 50%
54. Go on a space mission
55. Sonora; Chihuahua; Coahuila
56. United Mexican States
57. Green; white; red
58. President
59. Executive; legislative; judicial
60. Six years
61. Feliz Navidad
62. Las Posadas
63. Inn or lodging
64. False: 73% live in cities
65. Uno, dos, tres, cuatro, cinco, seis, siete, ocho, nueve, diez
66. Lake Chapala
67. Outdoor market
68. A person must gain official permission from the government
69. Nap or sleep
70. Adíos, amigo

North to Canada

This game has 50 questions about the history, geography, people, and places of Canada. Play the game with the entire class in teams or play with small groups using the rules below.

Purpose: to practice and review facts about Canada.

Materials Needed:

- card stock of any color to print game cards and to mount rules and answer key
- laminating material

Construction:

1. Print the game card pages on colored card stock. Laminate the pages, then cut cards apart.
2. Trim the rules and answer key boxes. Mount on card stock of the same color as used for game cards. Laminate them.

Rules for "North to Canada"

This game is for three or four players and one judge.

1. Judge shuffles the cards and spreads cards face down.

2. Player to judge's left goes first. Play moves to the left.

3. First player: Take a card and read card number and question aloud. Attempt to answer the question. The judge tells if the answer is correct.

4. Players earn points by keeping cards for questions they have answered correctly. When a player incorrectly answers a question, the judge reads the correct answer and the card is shuffled back into the card pile to be used again.

5. Play is over when all cards have been used or when game time is over. Player having the most cards is the winner.

---

1. Canada is the second largest country in the world. Which country is larger?	**2.** The Trans-Canada Highway is the longest continuous road on earth. How long is it?
3. In 1497, an Italian explorer, sailing for England, explored the Atlantic coast of Canada and claimed the land for England. Name this explorer.	**4.** What French explorer discovered the Gulf of St. Lawrence in 1534?
5. What French explorer founded Quebec in 1608?	**6.** When do Canadians celebrate Thanksgiving?
7. In 1873, Canada founded an organization to keep law and order in the country. This organization still exists today. Name it.	**8.** Two Canadians, Dr. Frederick Banting and Dr. Charles Best, discovered a substance that has saved the lives of many diabetics. What is this substance?
9. Canadian author Lucy Maud Montgomery wrote a book about an orphan girl growing up on Prince Edward Island. This book became a popular classic in America. Name the book.	**10.** Name the Canadian who invented the telephone in 1876.

11.

Ten U.S. states touch Canada's southern border. Name five of these states.

12.

Canada has ten provinces and two territories. Name the two largest provinces. Name one territory.

13.

What is the capital of Canada? In what province is this capital city found?

14.

The U.S. Congress meets in the Capitol Building. In what building does Canada's government meet and in what city is it found?

15.

What major waterway of Canada connects the Great Lakes with the Atlantic Ocean?

16.

Canada's two largest cities are in the province of Ontario. Name these two cities.

17.

Canada has five main landform regions. Name the largest of these.

18.

Canada's third largest city is in the western province of British Columbia. Name this city.

19.

What are the two official languages of Canada?

20.

Although England claimed the land, Canada was settled mostly by people from what country?

21.

In 1759, France and England fought their last great battle in North America. Which country won this battle and gained the right to rule the area that later became Canada?

22.

In 1867, Canada officially became a country. On what month and day does Canada celebrate its birthday?

23.

What official is the head of the government of Canada?

24.

Most public schools in Canada have how many grades?

25.

Students of Canadian schools start school in the month of _____ and get out in the month of _____.

26.

What is the national anthem of Canada?

27.

The head of the government of each state in the U.S. is the governor. What is the head official of each province of Canada?

28.

The U.S. is divided into 50 states. What are the divisions of Canada called?

29.

The largest Chinese community in North America is in San Francisco, California. The second largest Chinese community in North America is in the Canadian city of _____.

30.

What large island of Canada is found at the southwest end of British Columbia?

31.

Canada's two smallest provinces are islands. Name these two provinces.

32.

Name the huge bay that lies on the northern borders of the provinces of Quebec, Ontario, and Manitoba.

33.

What U.S. state borders British Columbia and the Yukon Territory?

34.

Only one of the Great Lakes does not touch Canada. Name this lake.

35.

Two Canadian cities often visited by tourists are Calgary and Edmonton. In what province are these cities found?

36.

What famous waterfall can be viewed from both the American side and the Canadian side?

37.

What popular sport has an International Hall of Fame in Kingston, Ontario?

38.

Canada is bordered by what ocean on the north?

39.

What is Canada's national emblem?

40.

What Canadian island would you visit to see a museum dedicated to the life and work of Alexander Graham Bell?

41.

An animal that lives in great numbers in Canada slaps the water with his tail to warn of approaching danger. Name this animal.

42.

West of the Northwest Territories is the huge Baffin Bay which separates Canada from the world's largest island. Name this island.

43.

The U.S. has four time zones. How many times zones lie within the borders of Canada?

44.

Only one province of Canada touches the Great Lakes. Name this province.

45.

The province of British Columbia is bordered by what ocean?

46.

Which country is the largest importer of Canada's forest products?

47.

What percentage of Canada's people live within 100 miles of the U.S. border?

48.

What major Indian group lives around the northern rim of North America?

49.

Nova Scotia was once a French colony called Acadia. Descendants of the Acadians migrated to Louisiana where they are known as _____.

50.

Canada's longest river is 2,635 miles long. Name this river.

Answer Key for "North to Canada"

1. Russia
2. Over 5,000 miles
3. John Cabot
4. Jacques Cartier
5. Samuel de Champlain
6. Second Monday in October
7. Royal Canadian Mounted Police
8. Insulin
9. *Anne of Green Gables*
10. Alexander Graham Bell
11. Washington, Idaho, Montana, North Dakota, Minnesota, Michigan, New York, Vermont, New Hampshire, and Maine
12. Largest provinces: Ontario and Quebec
    Territories: Yukon and Northwest Territories
13. Ottawa; Ontario
14. House of Parliament; Ottawa
15. St. Lawrence Seaway
16. Toronto and Montreal
17. Canadian Shield
18. Vancouver
19. English and French
20. France
21. England
22. July 1
23. Prime Minister
24. Twelve

25. September; June
26. "O Canada"
27. Premier
28. Provinces
29. Vancouver
30. Vancouver Island
31. Prince Edward Island and Nova Scotia
32. Hudson Bay
33. Alaska
34. Lake Michigan
35. Alberta
36. Niagara Falls
37. Hockey
38. Arctic Ocean
39. Maple leaf
40. Nova Scotia
41. Beaver
42. Greenland
43. Six
44. Ontario
45. Pacific Ocean
46. United States
47. 80%
48. Eskimos or Inuits
49. Cajuns
50. Mackenzie River

Meet the Presidents

This game has 150 questions, enough for several groups to play at the same time. Until the class is familiar with the presidents and the order in which they served, give each group a copy of the U.S. presidents chart to study.

Purpose: to learn facts about U.S. presidents

Materials Needed:

- card stock of any color to print game cards and the president chart and to mount rules
- laminating materials

Construction:

1. Print the game card pages and the presidents chart onto colored card stock. Laminate pages, then cut cards apart. The presidents chart can also be laminated.
2. Trim the rules box. Mount on same color as used for game cards. Laminate them. Note: If the game is to be used with several groups, make enough copies of the rules and the presidents chart for each group to have its own copy.

Rules for "Meet the Presidents"

This game is for three to four players and one scorekeeper. Pencil and paper are needed for keeping score.

1. Player to left of the scorekeeper goes first. Play moves to the left.
2. Scorekeeper shuffles cards and stacks the deck face down. The scorekeeper turns over the top card and reads a question to the first player.
3. Players earn points by keeping cards for questions they have answered correctly. When a player incorrectly answers a question, the card is shuffled back into the card pile to be used again.
4. When cards are gone, each player counts cards and the score for the round is recorded. Each card is worth one point.
5. Shuffle cards and play another round or trade cards with another group to answer new questions.
6. At the end of game time, total the scores from all rounds of play. Highest score wins!

United States Presidents

U.S. President	Term	Birth State	Wife's Name
1. George Washington	1789–1797	Virginia	Martha
2. John Adams	1797–1801	Massachusetts	Abigail
3. Thomas Jefferson	1801–1809	Virginia	Martha
4. James Madison	1809–1817	Virginia	Dolly
5. James Monroe	1817–1825	Virginia	Elizabeth
6. John Quincy Adams	1825–1829	Massachusetts	Louise
7. Andrew Jackson	1829–1837	South Carolina	Rachel
8. Martin Van Buren	1837–1841	New York	Hannah
9. William H. Harrison	1841	Virginia	Anna
10. John Tyler	1841–1845	Virginia	Letitia; Julia
11. James K. Polk	1845–1849	North Carolina	Sarah
12. Zachary Taylor	1849–1850	Virginia	Margaret
13. Millard Fillmore	1850–1853	New York	Abigail; Caroline
14. Franklin Pierce	1853–1857	New Hampshire	Jane
15. James Buchanan	1857–1861	Pennsylvania	(none)
16. Abraham Lincoln	1861–1865	Kentucky	Mary
17. Andrew Johnson	1865–1869	North Carolina	Eliza
18. Ulysses S. Grant	1869–1877	Ohio	Julia
19. Rutherford B. Hayes	1877–1881	Ohio	Lucy
20. James A. Garfield	1881	Ohio	Lucretia
21. Chester A. Arthur	1881–1885	Vermont	Ellen
22. Grover Cleveland	1885–1889	New Jersey	Frances
23. Benjamin Harrison	1889–1893	Ohio	Caroline; Mary
24. Grover Cleveland	1893–1897	New Jersey	Frances
25. William McKinley	1897–1901	Ohio	Ida
26. Theodore Roosevelt	1901–1909	New York	Alice; Edith
27. William H. Taft	1909–1913	Ohio	Helen
28. Woodrow Wilson	1913–1921	Virginia	Ellen; Edith
29. Warren G. Harding	1921–1923	Ohio	Florence
30. Calvin Coolidge	1923–1929	Vermont	Grace
31. Herbert Hoover	1929–1933	Iowa	Lou
32. Franklin D. Roosevelt	1933–1945	New York	Eleanor
33. Harry S. Truman	1945–1953	Missouri	Bess
34. Dwight D. Eisenhower	1953–1961	Texas	Mamie
35. John F. Kennedy	1961–1963	Massachusetts	Jacqueline
36. Lyndon B. Johnson	1963–1969	Texas	"Lady Bird"
37. Richard M. Nixon	1969–1974	California	Pat
38. Gerald Ford	1974–1977	Nebraska	Betty
39. James Earl Carter	1977–1981	Georgia	Rosalynn
40. Ronald Reagan	1981–1989	Illinois	Nancy
41. George Bush	1989–1993	Texas	Barbara
42. William Clinton	1993	Arkansas	Hillary

Which president was assassinated while he was watching a play at Ford's Theater in Washington, D.C.?

(Abraham Lincoln)

George Washington never lived in the White House. Why?

(The White House was not completed until the 2nd president's term.)

A committee decided what the Declaration of Independence would say, but a man who would later be president wrote the actual text. Name this man.

(Thomas Jefferson)

This president was related to 11 other presidents by birth or by marriage. He was in office longer than any other president. Name him.

(Franklin D. Roosevelt)

In 1861, this president became the first to receive a transcontinental telegram. Who was he?

(Abraham Lincoln)

The tenth president was the first president to get married while in office. However, he was not married at the White House. Name him.

(John Tyler)

This president was 6'4" tall—the tallest ever. Who was he?

(Abraham Lincoln)

This president stood at 5'4". He was the fourth president. Name him.

(James Madison)

Which man was the heaviest president ever to hold office? (His top weight was about 340 pounds.)

(William Howard Taft)

Name the only president who has held both the offices of U.S. President and Chief Justice of the Supreme Court.

(William Howard Taft)

At one time, long before he became president, he was sheriff of Erie County in New York. As sheriff, he hanged two men. Name this president.

(Grover Cleveland)

Only one president was ever married in the White House. Name this presidential bridegroom.

(Grover Cleveland)

Name the four presidents whose faces are carved in the rock at Mount Rushmore.

(George Washington, Thomas Jefferson, Abraham Lincoln, Theodore Roosevelt)

Which president is called the "Father of our Country?"

(George Washington)

Name a grandfather and grandson who both served as president.

(William H. Harrison and his grandson Benjamin Harrison)

Name a father and son who both served as president.

(John Adams and his son John Quincy Adams)

The fourth president helped to write the Bill of Rights. Name him.

(James Madison)

Which president was nicknamed "Old Hickory?"

(Andrew Jackson)

One president opened the White House to the public for his inaugural reception. In fact, the White House was nearly ruined by his wild parties. Name this president.

(Andrew Jackson)

One president kept a milk cow that grazed on the White House lawn. The cow's name was Pauline Wayne. Name this twenty-seventh president.

(William Howard Taft)

Which man was the only president elected to four terms? He died during his fourth term.

(Franklin D. Roosevelt)

A presidential election is held every four years in the month of _____.

(November)

On what month and date is the official swearing-in ceremony for the newly elected president?

(January 20)

Twenty-two of the first 42 presidents had this animal as a pet.

(Dog)

Who was the first president to take office because he was the vice-president when the president in office died?

(John Tyler)

The Civil War began in April of 1861. Who was U.S. President at this time?

(Abraham Lincoln)

Who became president when John Wilkes Booth shot and killed Abraham Lincoln?

(Andrew Johnson)

In 1833, a president rode on a railroad train for the first time. Name this president.

(Andrew Jackson)

The first president born outside the original 13 states was born in Kentucky in a log cabin. Name him.

(Abraham Lincoln)

In May of 1819, the president then in office became the first president to ride on a steamship. Name him.

(James Monroe)

You are visiting The Hermitage, the home of a former president. You are near Nashville, Tennessee. Which president's home are you visiting?

(Andrew Jackson)

John Adams was the first president to live in the White House. The next president was the first to be inaugurated in the city of Washington, D.C. Name this president.

(Thomas Jefferson)

The second president to be assassinated might have been saved if X-ray had been invented then. An X-ray could have helped to locate the bullet lodged near the president's spine. Which president was this?

(James Garfield)

Name the only president to be sworn into office by his father, a judge. This person became president after the death of President Warren G. Harding.

(Calvin Coolidge)

This president served the shortest term because he gave a long inauguration speech on a cold day, caught pneumonia, and died one month later.

(William Henry Harrison)

The president who served the shortest term was also the first to have his picture taken while in office. Name him.

(William Henry Harrison)

Which president talked so little that he gained the nickname "Silent Cal"?

(Calvin Coolidge)

Which president was the only president to be born on the Fourth of July. He was born in 1872 in Vermont.

(Calvin Coolidge)

Someone shot at this president, but his life was spared when the bullet struck his glasses case and a speech folded into his pocket. Name him.

(Theodore Roosevelt)

The first presidential assassination attempt took place in 1835 when the president was shot at with two pistols. Both misfired. Name the president.

(Andrew Jackson)

The first child born in the White House was the grandson of President _____.

(Thomas Jefferson)

California is the site of the presidential libraries of which two presidents?

(Richard Nixon; Ronald Reagan)

Before they became presidents, George Washington and James Madison helped to write what important document?

(U.S. Constitution)

This man entered a competition to draw a design for the president's house (The White House). He did not win, but later he became the second president to live in the White House. Name him.

(Thomas Jefferson)

The first president to be assassinated was Abraham Lincoln. Who was the second president to be assassinated in 1881?

(James Garfield)

He was the only president to be divorced and remarried at the time of his election; his first wife was actress Jane Wyman. Name him.

(Ronald Reagan)

The first outdoor wedding at the White House was held in its famous rose garden in 1971; the bride's name was Tricia. Who was her presidential father?

(Richard Nixon)

Only one president in U.S. history has resigned from office before his term ended. Name this president.

(Richard Nixon)

One president occasionally spoke Chinese with his wife, Lou, so others would not know what they were talking about. Name this president.

(Herbert Hoover)

This president's hometown was Kinderhook, New York. His nickname was "O.K.," short for "Old Kinderhook." Who was he?

(Martin Van Buren)

There has been only one bachelor president. He was once engaged, but his fiancee died tragically and he never married. Name him.

(James Buchanan)

The president's home has been called Executive Mansion, President's House, and President's Palace. It became the "White House" when the twenty-sixth president had this name put on his official stationery. Name this president.

(Theodore Roosevelt)

This president's parents gave him a middle initial "S" but no name because they did not want to offend the grandfathers, whose names both began with an S. Name this president.

(Harry Truman)

Which president was a Hollywood movie star before he became president?

(Ronald Reagan)

Name the only president who served two non-consecutive terms, as the 22nd and the 24th president.

(Grover Cleveland)

One president had five children and many "presidential pets" including dogs, cats, rabbits, guinea pigs, squirrels, raccoons, a badger, a bear, a kangaroo, a rat, a snake, a parrot, and a pony. Name this presidential father.

(Theodore Roosevelt)

Which president was in office when the U.S. entered World War I?

(Woodrow Wilson)

Which president was in office when Japan bombed Pearl Harbor and the U.S. entered World War II?

(Franklin Roosevelt)

Which president made the decision to drop atom bombs on Japan in an effort to end World War II?

(Harry Truman)

When this president was running for office, his popular campaign slogan was "I Like Ike." Name this president.

(Dwight D. Eisenhower)

This president from Georgia was once a commander of a nuclear submarine. He became a peanut farmer before he was a politician. Name him.

(Jimmy Carter)

Most U.S. coins have faces of presidents on them. Whose face appears on the penny?

(Abraham Lincoln)

Eight daughters of presidents have had White House weddings. Only the son of the sixth president was married in the White House. Name the sixth president.

(John Quincy Adams)

Name the president first elected to office in 1992 and his home state.

(Bill Clinton, Arkansas)

Which president was in office during "Operation Desert Storm," in which the U.S. and other countries stopped Iraq from taking over Kuwait?

(George Bush)

Most U.S. coins have faces of presidents on them. Whose face appears on the nickel?

(Thomas Jefferson)

On which U.S. monetary bill does the face of George Washington appear?

(One dollar bill)

Most U.S. coins have faces of presidents on them. Whose face appears on the dime?

(Franklin D. Roosevelt)

Most U.S. coins have faces of presidents on them. Whose face appears on a silver dollar?

(Dwight D. Eisenhower)

Three presidents' faces appear on both dollars and coins. Name these three presidents.

(George Washington, Thomas Jefferson, and Abraham Lincoln)

Six presidents have shared the same first name. What is this popular name?

(James)

Name the president who was assassinated while riding in a motorcade in Dallas, Texas.

(John F. Kennedy)

Both Abraham Lincoln and John Kennedy were assassinated while in office. There were two others. Name them.

(James Garfield and William McKinley)

In July, 1969, U.S. astronaut Neil Armstrong became the first man to step from a spaceship onto the surface of the moon. Who was president at the time?

(Richard Nixon)

Central heating was installed in the White House during the term of the fourteenth president. Name this president.

(Franklin Pierce)

This president refused to move into the White House until an 81-year accumulation of shabby furniture was removed. Name this twenty-first president.

(Chester A. Arthur)

Which president was involved in the break-in at the Watergate Hotel?

(Richard Nixon)

The Whitewater scandal occurred during which president's administration?

(Bill Clinton)

Who was president when the Statue of Liberty was presented to the U.S. by France?

(Grover Cleveland)

The Wright Brothers made the first successful airplane flight at Kitty Hawk, North Carolina, in 1903. Name the president who was in office.

(Theodore Roosevelt)

The annual Easter egg roll was held at the U.S. Capitol until the First Lady, Lucy, had it moved to the White House during her husband's term. Name the president to whom Lucy was married.

(Rutherford B. Hayes)

What is the correct way to start a letter to the president of the United States?

("Dear Mr. President")

What is the address of the White House?

(1600 Pennsylvania Avenue, Washington, D.C.)

He won three varsity letters playing football for the University of Michigan. Name this thirty-eighth president.

(Gerald Ford)

Name the only man who served as both vice-president and president without being elected to either office.

(Gerald Ford)

In the late 1940s, the White House was in danger of falling. The interior was taken apart and completely rebuilt. The president and his family lived in another house during this renovation. Who was president at the time?

(Harry Truman)

Across the street from the White House is a guest house used by dignitaries who have come to visit the president. What is the name of this guest house?

(Blair House)

In Maryland, there is a presidential retreat where the president may go to rest and relax. Name this presidential retreat.

(Camp David)

One large president got stuck in the White House bath tub. Secret service agents had to pull him out. He ordered a new tub that could hold four men. Who was he?

(William Howard Taft)

In Washington, D.C., you can see Daniel Chester French's statue of this famous president sitting in solemn thought. Name the president.

(Abraham Lincoln)

The eighteenth, nineteenth, and twentieth presidents were born in Ohio and were also generals in the Civil War. Name them.

(Ulysses S. Grant, Rutherford B. Hayes, and James A. Garfield)

Before becoming president, he was John Kennedy's vice president.   He also owned two beagles named Him and Her. Name this president.

(Lyndon B. Johnson)

One state is known as the "Mother of Presidents" because eight presidents were born there. Name this state.

(Virginia)

Jefferson Davis, the president of the Confederate States of America during the Civil War, was the son-in-law of the twelfth president. Name this president.

(Zachary Taylor)

Jackie was a newspaper reporter before her marriage. She became First Lady when her husband became president. To whom was she married?

(John F. Kennedy)

Alexander Graham Bell invented the telephone in 1876. Who was president?

(Ulysses S. Grant)

This president's secretary, Sarah, was also his wife. Name this eleventh president.

(James K. Polk)

He was the first president to be married to a college graduate. His wife, Lucy, graduated from college in 1850 with highest honors. Who was this president?

(Rutherford B. Hayes)

He was the first president to be married to a college graduate. His wife, Lucy, graduated from college in 1850 with highest honors. Who was this president?

One president was a tailor by trade and custom-made all of his clothing while he was president. Who was this seventeenth president?

(Andrew Johnson)

Only one president has ever been impeacheds or accused of wrongdoings by the House of Representatives. The Senate found this president "not guilty" by one vote. Name him.

(Andrew Johnson)

This president was the first to have an automobile at the White House. Name this twenty-seventh president.

(William Howard Taft)

In 1921, a president rode to his inauguration in an automobile for the first time. Name this president from Ohio.

(Warren G. Harding)

One First Lady was known as "Lemonade Lucy" because she allowed nothing stronger than lemonade to be served at the White House. Name her husband.

(Rutherford B. Hayes)

The Gettysburg Address was a two-minute speech to dedicate Gettysburg Battlefield as a memorial cemetery for Civil War soldiers who died there. Who gave his famous speech?

(Abraham Lincoln)

One famous presidential dog was Fala, a Scottie. Fala's owner was president during almost all of World War II. Name this president.

(Franklin D. Roosevelt)

One president received a Pulitzer Prize for his book of short biographies of great men entitled *Profiles in Courage*. Name this president.

(John F. Kennedy)

Only one First Lady has ever been pictured on U.S. currency. Her face was on the one-dollar silver certificate issued in September, 1886. Name this first lady.

(Martha Washington)

The first president to travel outside the U.S. during his term in office visited Panama to see the progress on the Panama Canal. Name this president.

(Theodore Roosevelt)

He was the first president to ride in an automobile (1902), to submerge in a submarine (1905), and, as an ex-president, to fly in an airplane (1910). Name this president.

(Theodore Roosevelt)

This president was known as "Old Rough and Ready." He died after being in office only a little more than a year. Name him.

(Zachary Taylor)

Electric lights were installed in the White House in 1890. However, the president and his family were afraid to use them and servants had to turn the lights on and off. Name this grandson of the ninth president.

(Benjamin Harrison)

The War of 1812 was fought between the U.S. and the British. During this war, the British burned the White House. Who was president at the time?

(James Madison)

The tenth president was the father of 15 children, more than any other president. Who was this president?

(John Tyler)

This president was the only one ever to be sworn in on an airplane as well as by a female judge in November, 1963, in Dallas, Texas. Name this president.

(Lyndon B. Johnson)

The first woman cabinet officer was Francis Perkins, who was made Secretary of Labor in 1933. Which president appointed her?

(Franklin D. Roosevelt)

This president was the first person in North America to grow tomatoes, which people at the time thought to be poisonous. He has invented many useful items, such as the weather vane. Name him.

(Thomas Jefferson)

In this president's home, Monticello, you can see many of his inventions. Name this president.

(Thomas Jefferson)

Mount Vernon, Virginia, is the home of which president?

(George Washington)

Two presidents were elected to Congress after being president. The sixth president served in the House; the seventh served in the Senate. Name these two men.

(John Quincy Adams and Andrew Johnson)

Only two presidents are buried in Arlington National Cemetery. One is William Howard Taft. Name the other president.

(John F. Kennedy)

In 1850, this president's wife refused to move into the White House until Congress agreed to spend the money to have a bathtub installed. Name the president.

(Millard Fillmore)

This president was a famous Civil War General, but he was not a music lover. He said, "I only know two tunes. One of them is 'Yankee Doodle' and the other one isn't." Who was he?

(Ulysses S. Grant)

This president had a sign on his desk that said, "The buck stops here." This means that he believed what happened to the country was his responsibility. Who was this president?

(Harry Truman)

This president was often teased because of his clumsiness. He once drove a golf ball that hit a spectator in the head. He was the thirty-eighth president. Name him.

(Gerald Ford)

This First Lady gained such fame as a hostess of lovely parties that a modern-day line of bakery goods has been named for her. Who was she?

(Dolley Madison)

John F. Kennedy said, "Ask not what your country can do for you, ask what you can do for your country." But these are not his words; he borrowed them from the twenty-ninth president. Name this twenty-ninth president.

(Warren G. Harding)

One president had a cross-eyed wife, Julia. He didn't want her to have surgery to correct the problem because he said he liked her that way. Name this eighteenth president.

(Ulysses S. Grant)

This president became the first to appear on TV on April 30, 1939, at the opening of the World's Fair. Who was he?

(Franklin D. Roosevelt)

He could write Greek with one hand and Latin with the other hand—at the same time! He was the second president to die from an assassin's bullet. Name him.

(James Garfield)

One first lady got into trouble with Congress because she ran up a $27,000 clothing bill. Her husband never knew. He died first, murdered by John Wilkes Booth. Name him.

(Abraham Lincoln)

More presidents have been Episcopalians than any other religion. Name the only Roman Catholic who has served as president.

(John F. Kennedy)

One president suffered from acromegaly, a growth hormone disorder that caused him to be unusually tall. Name this president.

(Abraham Lincoln)

This president had polio at age 26 and spent the rest of his life in a wheelchair. He was able to stand only with locked leg braces. Name him.

(Franklin D. Roosevelt)

Only one president has ever been married at the White House. His bride's name was Frances Folsom and the wedding was in 1886. Name this president.

(Grover Cleveland)

One president's history was partially lost when his son burned his private papers. Name this thirteenth president.

(Millard Fillmore)

Who was president when the vast Louisiana Territory was purchased from France in 1803?

(Thomas Jefferson)

The forty-ninth and fiftieth states, Alaska and Hawaii, both came into the Union in 1959. Who was president in that year?

(Dwight D. Eisenhower)

Two men helped to write the Declaration of Independence and then later became president. Both men died on the same day, July 4, 1826—the 50th anniversary of the Declaration of Independence. Name these men.

(John Adams and Thomas Jefferson)

One president enjoyed playing the piano, especially the song of his state, "The Missouri Waltz." Name this president.

(Harry Truman)

Which president was the first to fly in an airplane while he was in office?

(Franklin D. Roosevelt)

Margaret, the only child of the only president from Missouri, called the White House "The Great White Jail." Who was her president father?

(Harry Truman)

Which president was a five-star general and commander of all allied forces in Europe during World War II before becoming president?

(Dwight D. Eisenhower)

The name Chelsea has been used for only one president's daughter. Name Chelsea's father.

(Bill Clinton)

This president from Missouri loved the opening day of baseball season. He could show off by throwing the ball out with either hand. Name him.

(Harry Truman)

Until he became president in 1850, White House cooking was done over an open fire. This president purchased a cast iron stove and taught the cook how to use it. Who was he?

(Millard Fillmore)

In 1947, he was the first president to broadcast a speech over TV from the White House. Who was this president?

(Harry Truman)

This president's wife wrote a book about her very popular dog, Millie. Name this First Lady.

(Barbara Bush)

When he visited China, reporters asked him how he liked the Great Wall of China. His answer: "I must say that the Great Wall is a great wall." Name this thirty-seventh president.

(Richard Nixon)

One president's wife, Lou, once served as President of the Girl Scouts of America. Who was Lou's president husband?

(Herbert Hoover)

First Lady Agatha had to live in an unfinished White House. She even used the East Room as a place to hang drying clothes. Name Agatha's husband, the first president to live in the White House.

(John Adams)

America, America

This game has 180 cards, with 30 cards each on six different topics with an American slant: people, symbols, parks and monuments, rivers and bodies of water, states, and government. Each set of cards must be printed on a different color card stock in order to play the game correctly.

Purpose: to practice and review knowledge about the U.S.

Materials Needed:
- card stock in the following colors: pink, green, yellow, blue, white, and orange
- laminating materials

Construction:
1. Print the game card pages onto card stock according to the color indicated on each page. Laminate the pages, then cut the cards apart. If for any reason you must print the game cards on stock other than the colors indicated, you will need to change the rules and scoring for the game.
2. Make six copies of the rules box and trim them before mounting them on card stock that corresponds in color to the appropriate game cards. Laminate.
3. Cut out the answer key boxes. Answer key boxes should be mounted on card stock that corresponds in color to the appropriate game cards. Trim and laminate the answer keys.

 Rules for "America, America"

Play Variations:

1. Divide the class into six groups. Each group gets a set of questions with the appropriate answer key. For a correct answer, the player keeps the card. If the answer is incorrect, the card is returned to the card pile. When all cards are used, the player having the most cards is the winner. Groups then trade cards and play again. Be sure to make six copies of the rules so that each group gets one.

2. Use the game with the entire class. Divide the class into groups of four. Each group should appoint one person to be the spokesperson. Give each group a number. Shuffle cards in separate decks by color. Lay the decks of cards face down in a horizontal row. Write the categories and point values on board as follows:

Number of Points	Card Color	Category
2	Yellow	The Fifty States
2	Blue	Rivers and Bodies of Water
3	Green	U.S. Symbols
3	White	U.S. Government
4	Pink	Famous People
4	Orange	National Sites

You will also need to create a chart to keep a tally of team scores.

Allow the first group the first chance to answer the question from a card from its chosen category, with the spokesperson standing and giving the group's answer. If the group answers correctly, give them the correct number of points. If the group answers incorrectly, deduct points and go on to the next group. Continue in this way until a question is answered correctly. If, however, no group knows the answer, the game leader tells the correct answer and the card goes to the bottom of the stack to be used again.

Make six copies of the rules on card stock.

Rules for "America, America"

This game is for three to four players and one judge. Paper and pencil are needed to keep score. Judge holds the answer keys.

1. Judge shuffles the cards in decks separated by color. Judge places the decks in a horizontal row, face down, in center of table.

2. Player to judge's left goes first. Play moves to the left.

3. First player takes a card from any deck. Player reads the card number and the question aloud. Player attempts to answer the question.

4. Judge tells if the answer is correct and records the score.

2 points

    Yellow: The Fifty States

    Blue: Rivers & Bodies of Water

3 points

    Green: U.S. Symbols

    White: U.S. Government

4 points

    Pink: Famous People

    Orange: National Sites

5. Judge scores as follows:

   Correct answer: Appropriate number of points are added to score. Put card in a discard stack. Next player's turn.

   Incorrect answer: Appropriate number of points are deducted from score. Put the card at the bottom of the stack to be used again. Next player's turn.

6. When all cards are used or game time is over, the player who has the highest score is the winner.

Copy these cards onto **yellow** card stock.

1.

Name the only New England state that has a connecting border with only one other state.

2.

Frankfort is the capital of the state of _____.

3.

To what city and state would you travel to see the Golden Gate Bridge?

4.

In which U.S. city and state is the United Nations located?

5.

Which state is the U.S.'s leading producer of potatoes?

6.

Americans first tasted hot dogs and ice cream at the 1904 World's Fair. Name the city and the state where this World's Fair was held.

7.

The world's largest volcano is located in which of the fifty states?

8.

The popular board game "Monopoly" has street names based on a New Jersey city. Name this city.

9.

Harvard, America's oldest university, is located in the city and state of _____.

10.

The oldest city in the U.S. is located in the city and state of _____.

11.

"City of Angels" is the nickname for the city of _____ in the state of _____.

12.

Which city in Tennessee has the world's only museum dedicated to the study of the atom?

13.

The first U.S. shopping center, "The Plaza," opened in 1922 in _____, Missouri.

14.

The capital of Tennessee is known as the "country music capital of the world." Name this city.

15.

Which state is the geographical center of the contiguous U.S.?

16.

Which state is named for the longest river in the U.S.?

17.

NASA, the U.S. Space Headquarters, is located in what city and state?

18.

Which state is called the "Grand Canyon State"?

19.

To which state would one travel if one wanted to visit Death Valley?

20.

"Motor City, U.S.A." is the place to see late-model cars. What city and state is it in?

21.

The most famous ship of early America, "Old Ironsides," is located in what city and state?

22.

The abbreviations for the states beginning with M are confusing. Name four of the following states that begin with the letter M: MA, ME, MD, MI, MN, MO, MS, MT.

23.

The territory that became the state of _____ was purchased from Russia in 1867.

24.

To which state must you go if you want to visit the famous Black Hills?

25.

The first railroad to cross America was built from the east and from the west. The two parts were joined by a golden spike in 1869. Name the city and state where the golden spike was driven into the ground to finish this railroad.

26.

Which state produces more butter and cheese than any other state?

27.

Niagara Falls is one of America's favorite honeymoon spots. In which state is Niagara Falls?

28.

Name the capital of California.

29.

Which two states are the birthplaces of more U.S. presidents than any other states?

30.

Which U.S. president has both a city and a state named for him?

Trim and mount the answer key below on **yellow** card stock.

Answer Key for "America, America"

(Yellow Deck)

1. Maine

2. Kentucky

3. San Francisco, California

4. New York, New York

5. Idaho

6. St. Louis, Missouri

7. Hawaii

8. Atlantic City

9. Cambridge, Massachusetts

10. St. Augustine, Florida

11. Los Angeles, California

12. Oak Ridge

13. Kansas City

14. Nashville

15. Kansas

16. Mississippi

17. Houston, Texas

18. Arizona

19. California

20. Detroit, Michigan

21. Boston, Massachusetts

22. Massachusetts, Maine, Maryland, Michigan, Minnesota, Missouri, Mississippi, Montana

23. Alaska

24. South Dakota

25. Promontory Point, Utah

26. Wisconsin

27. New York

28. Sacramento

29. Ohio and Virginia

30. George Washington

Copy these cards onto **blue** card stock.

1.

The Grand Canyon was formed over millions of years as rock and soil were eroded away by the _____ River.

2.

What river forms the border between Oregon and Washington?

3.

Only one of the Great Lakes lies totally within the U.S. Name this lake.

4.

Which one of the Great Lakes is the second largest lake in the world?

5.

There is a lake in the U.S. which contains a greater percentage of salt than either the Atlantic or the Pacific Ocean. Name this lake.

6.

The Great Salt Lake is in which state?

7.

Which U.S. river has been nicknamed "Old Man River"?

8.

What is the longest river in the U.S.?

9.

Into what body of the water does the Mississippi River empty?

10.

Alaska is the only state that is bordered by two oceans. Name these two oceans.

Copy these cards onto **blue** card stock.

11. Name the river that flows through the national capital of our country.	**12.** The Missouri River empties into the Mississippi River at what large U.S. city?
13. What river flows southwest from Pittsburgh, Pennsylvania, and empties into the Mississippi River at Cairo, Illinois?	**14.** There is a U.S. lake that is named for the French explorer Samuel de Champlain. This lake forms a boundary between the states of Vermont and New York. Name this lake.
15. The highest bridge in the U.S. is the Royal Gorge Suspension Bridge. Which river in Colorado is crossed by this bridge?	**16.** The famous Brooklyn Bridge crosses the East River in what U.S. city?
17. George Washington's Virginia home, Mount Vernon, stands on the banks of what river?	**18.** Name the largest bay on the U.S. Atlantic coast.
19. What happens to the rainwater that drains into the Great Salt Lake? Why?	**20.** The western boundary of Texas is formed by what river?

Copy these cards onto **blue** card stock.

21.

Which is the smallest of the Great Lakes?

22.

Name the river that runs all the way across Arizona, east to west, and then empties into the Colorado River.

23.

The triangle-shaped deposit of silt at the mouth of the Mississippi River is called the Mississippi _____.

24.

What river forms most of the western boundary of the state of Arizona?

25.

What lake in Minnesota is the headwater of the Mississippi River?

26.

What river is the largest tributary of the Mississippi?

27.

What water route connects the Great Lakes and the Atlantic Ocean?

28.

What word is a memory device to help you remember the names of the five Great Lakes?

29.

What percentage of the Great Salt Lake is salt?

30.

The Colorado River empties into what body of water?

Trim and mount the answer key below on **blue** card stock.

Answer Key for "America, America"

(Blue Deck)

1. Colorado
2. Columbia River
3. Lake Michigan
4. Lake Superior
5. Great Salt Lake
6. Utah
7. Mississippi River
8. Mississippi River
9. Gulf of Mexico
10. Arctic Ocean; Pacific Ocean
11. Potomac River
12. St. Louis
13. Ohio River
14. Lake Champlain
15. Arkansas River
16. New York City
17. Potomac River
18. Chesapeake Bay
19. It evaporates; the lake has no outlet.
20. Rio Grande
21. Lake Ontario
22. Gila River (pronounced hee-la)
23. Delta
24. Colorado River
25. Lake Itasca
26. Missouri River
27. St. Lawrence Seaway
28. HOMES: Huron, Ontario, Michigan, Erie, Superior
29. 25%
30. Gulf of California

Copy these cards onto **green** card stock.

1. The "Star Spangled Banner" was inspired by the view of the American flag waving over Fort McHenry. Where does this flag hang today?	**2.** During what war was the "Star Spangled Banner" written?
3. What is the national bird of the U.S.?	**4.** The bald eagle's head is covered with white feathers. Why is it called the "bald" eagle?
5. The Great Seal of the United States is used for _____.	**6.** Benjamin Franklin did not think the eagle was a good choice for a national bird. What bird did he suggest?
7. On the Great Seal of the United States, there are 13 stars above the eagle's head. What do these 13 stars represent?	**8.** The official library of the United States government is the _____ located in Washington, D.C.
9. Who laid the original cornerstone of the United States Capitol Building?	**10.** In 1959, President _____ laid the cornerstone for the expansion of the United States Capitol.

Copy these cards onto **green** card stock.

11. In 1886, President Grover Cleveland dedicated the world's most famous statue. Name this statue.	**12.** Where can you go to see the Statue of Liberty?
13. How did the U.S. get the Statue of Liberty?	**14.** Whose face was used as a model for the face on the Statue of Liberty?
15. "Uncle Sam" is a nickname for the U.S. government. It first came into use during which war?	**16.** On July 20, 1956, Congress adopted an official motto for the United States. What is this motto?
17. How many stars are on the U.S. flag? Why?	**18.** In a forest in Maryland there is a presidential retreat where the president can go to rest and relax. Name this presidential retreat.
19. One famous U.S. symbol is imprinted with these words from the Bible: "Proclaim liberty throughout all the land unto all the inhabitants thereof." Name this symbol.	**20.** Name the flag maker of Baltimore, Maryland, who made the flag that inspired the writing of the "Star Spangled Banner."

Copy these cards onto **green** card stock.

21.

In July 1835, the Liberty Bell rang upon the death of Chief Justice John Marshall. What happened to the bell at that time?

22.

What famous tourist attraction was shipped to the U.S. in 214 crates and took over a year to assemble?

23.

Although this fictitious person first came into use during the War of 1812, Congress did not make him an official national symbol until 1961. Name this symbol.

24.

Francis Bellamy, an editor-writer for "The Youth's Companion" "magazine, wrote the _____ in 1892 to help honor the 400th anniversary of Columbus's discovery of America.

25.

The _____ was ordered from England by the colonists who lived in Pennsylvania. It arrived in this country in 1752.

26.

To what city and state would you go to see the Liberty Bell?

27.

The "purple heart" is a medal awarded to members of the U.S. armed forces. Why is this award given?

28.

After the death of a U.S. president, the flag flies at half-mast for _____ days.

29.

The Old Admiral's House is on 10 acres of land at the U.S. Naval Observatory. What U.S. official lives in this house?

30.

What does the U.S. Flag Code specify?

Trim and mount the answer key below on **green** card stock.

Answer Key for "America, America"

(Green Deck)

1. Museum of American History, Smithsonian Institution

2. War of 1812

3. Bald eagle

4. "Balde" was the old English word for white; "balde eagle" later became "bald eagle."

5. Stamping official government documents

6. Turkey

7. The 13 original colonies

8. Library of Congress

9. George Washington

10. Dwight Eisenhower

11. Statue of Liberty

12. Liberty Island, New York

13. It was a gift from France to symbolize the friendship between the two countries.

14. Frederick Bartholdi, the sculptor, used his mother's face as the model for the Statue of Liberty.

15. War of 1812

16. "In God We Trust"

17. 50; they represent the states

18. Camp David

19. Liberty Bell

20. Mary Pickersgill

21. The bell cracked

22. Statue of Liberty

23. Uncle Sam

24. Pledge of Allegiance

25. Liberty Bell

26. Philadelphia, Pennsylvania

27. For injury or death in combat

28. Thirty

29. Vice President

30. How citizens should display and care for the flag

Copy these cards onto **white** card stock.

1. What is the title of the person who presides over the Senate? What is the title of the person who presides over the House of Representatives?	**2.** Who is the current Speaker of the House? What state does the Speaker represent?
3. Name the two senators who represent your state in Congress.	**4.** In which federal Congressional District do you live? Who is your representative to the House of Representatives?
5. A person who comes to this country from France and wants to become a U.S. citizen can do this by going through the process of _____.	**6.** How many states must agree to a Constitutional amendment before it can be added to the Constitution?
7. Name the two houses of Congress.	**8.** What is the name of the building in which Congress meets?
9. Only one amendment has been added to the Constitution and then repealed. What was the purpose of this amendment?	**10.** Who is the President of the United States? Who is the Vice President?

11.

How old must a person be if he or she wants to run for a seat in the House of Representatives? In the Senate?

12.

How old must a person be if he or she wants to run for President of the United States?

13.

True or False: Only a natural-born American citizen can become President of the United States.

14.

On what month and date after election does a newly-elected president officially take office?

15.

What do we call the day on which a newly-elected President is sworn in and officially takes office?

16.

What official of the U.S. government is the Commander-In-Chief of the U.S. Armed Forces?

17.

What is the highest court in America? How many justices serve on this court?

18.

Name the Chief Justice of the U.S. Supreme Court.

19.

When the House of Representatives charges a president with crimes, this is called _____.

20.

If the House of Representatives charges a president with crimes, a trial is held in the _____.

Copy these cards onto **white** card stock.

21.

What are the first 10 amendments to the U.S. Constitution called?

22.

What is the official title of the wife of the president of the United States?

23.

How long is one term for a U.S. Senator? How long is one term for a member of the House of Representatives?

24.

Name the three branches of the Federal Government.

25.

How many members are in the Senate? In the House of Representatives?

26.

How many amendments have been added to the U.S. Constitution?

27.

The 26th amendment to the U.S. Constitution affects someone when he or she becomes 18 years old. What does this amendment say?

28.

In 1981, Sandra Day O'Connor became the first woman to serve on the Supreme Court. Which president appointed her?

29.

Who must sign a bill passed by Congress before that bill can become a law?

30.

When the President refuses to sign a bill passed by Congress, this is called the presidential _____.

Trim and mount the answer key below on **white** card stock.

Answer Key for "America, America"

(White Deck)

1. Vice President of the U.S.; Speaker of the House

2. Answers will vary.

3. Answers will vary.

4. Answers will vary.

5. Naturalization

6. 3/4 of the 50 states

7. Senate; House of Representatives

8. The U.S. Capitol Building

9. To prohibit the sale of alcoholic beverages (18th amendment)

10. Answers will vary.

11. Age 25; age 30

12. Age 35

13. True

14. January 20

15. Inauguration Day

16. President of the United States

17. U.S. Supreme Court; nine

18. Answers will vary.

19. Impeachment

20. Senate

21. The Bill of Rights

22. First Lady

23. Six years; two years

24. Executive branch; legislative branch; judicial branch

25. Senate has 100; House of Representatives has 435

26. There are 27 amendments.

27. It gives 18-year-olds the right to vote.

28. President Ronald Reagan

29. The President

30. Veto

Note: Items 2, 3, 4, 10 and 18 have been left blank so that you can fill in the appropriate answers.

Copy these cards onto **orange** card stock.

1. In which national park can you see America's tallest waterfall? Name the waterfall.	**2.** The tallest man-made monument in the U.S. is 630 feet tall and overlooks a river. Name the monument and tell the city and state in which it is located.
3. A popular monument was built in St. Louis, Missouri, to symbolize "the gateway to the west." Name this monument.	**4.** A popular monument in Washington, D.C. was begun in 1848 to honor one of our presidents. It took 36 years to complete it. Name this monument.
5. The first geographical landmark to be declared a National Monument by Congress is located in Wyoming. Name this monument.	**6.** Where would you go to see the place where the famous Battle of the Alamo took place?
7. In Washington, D.C., there is a memorial built of black granite that honors those who died in the _____ War.	**8.** Name America's first national park.
9. During the Civil War, the northern government took over Robert E. Lee's home in Virginia. This site became what national memorial?	**10.** To which state would you go to visit Badlands National Park?

Copy these cards onto **orange** card stock.

11.

To which state would you go to visit the Petrified Forest National Park?

12.

True or False: In the Smithsonian Institution's National Museum of American Art you can only see art works done by American artists.

13.

What is so special about the Saguaro Cactus that a National Monument was set up to protect it?

14.

In what state is the Saguaro Cactus National Monument located?

15.

The Roosevelt Arch is located at the main entrance of which national park?

16.

Mount Rushmore is a mountain carving of which four presidents? In which state is Mount Rushmore located?

17.

What building, in what city, would you visit to see the original copies of the U.S. Constitution and the Declaration of Independence?

18.

What is the street address of the White House?

19.

In Idaho there is a national monument that is so desolate and lifeless that it has been used as a training area for astronauts who will travel to the moon. Name this national monument.

20.

Skyline Drive in Shenandoah National Park is located in the state of _____.

21.

Mammoth Cave National Park has over 150 miles of caves and is thought to be over 340 million years old. What state does one visit to see this park?

22.

Near Colorado Springs, Colorado, there is a famous mountain that is over 14,000 feet tall. Name this mountain.

23.

We are traveling along the Oregon Trail. Three landmarks tell us how far we have come—Scott's Bluff, Courthouse Rock, and Chimney Rock. All of these are located in what present-day state?

24.

At Disney World in Florida, one of the main attractions is EPCOT Center. What does EPCOT stand for?

25.

The Great Smoky Mountains National Park spans across two states. Name these two states.

26.

Twenty-six glaciers originate at or near the top of Mount Rainier. In which state is Mount Rainier located?

27.

In the U.S. Capitol Building, there is a statue of President Lincoln that is missing an ear. Why did the sculptor do this?

28.

What famous memorial in Washington, D.C., was dedicated on the 200th birthday anniversary of President Thomas Jefferson?

29.

Carlsbad Caverns National Park is in the state of _____.

30.

During one president's term, the White House was torn down, except for the exterior walls, and rebuilt. The president and his family had to move out during the renovation. Name this president.

Trim and mount the answer key below on **orange** card stock.

Answer Key for "America, America"

(Orange Deck)

1. Yosemite National Park; Yosemite Falls

2. Gateway Arch; St. Louis, Missouri

3. Gateway Arch

4. Washington Monument

5. Devil's Tower

6. San Antonio, Texas

7. Vietnam

8. Yellowstone National Park

9. Arlington National Cemetery

10. South Dakota

11. Arizona

12. True

13. The Saguaro Cactus is the largest species of cactus in the world.

14. Arizona

15. Yellowstone

16. George Washington, Thomas Jefferson, Abraham Lincoln, and Theodore Roosevelt; South Dakota

17. The National Archives Building, Washington, D.C.

18. 1600 Pennsylvania Avenue

19. Craters of the Moon National Monument

20. Virginia

21. Kentucky

22. Pike's Peak

23. Nebraska

24. Experimental Prototype Community of Tomorrow

25. North Carolina and Tennessee

26. Washington

27. To symbolize Lincoln's unfinished life

28. Jefferson Memorial

29. New Mexico

30. President Harry Truman

Copy these cards onto **pink** card stock.

1.

Who invented the light bulb, the phonograph, and other inventions?

2.

Name the man wrote the text of the Declaration of Independence and later became the third president of the United States.

3.

A famous patriot of the American Revolution was hanged by the British for spying. Just before he died he said, "I only regret that I have but one life to lose for my country." Name this patriot.

4.

Name the doctor who developed the first vaccine to protect against polio.

5.

Name the person who founded the American Red Cross.

6.

What "first" was accomplished in Wyoming by Nellie Taylor Ross in 1924?

7.

Who was the first American astronaut to go into outer space?

8.

Name the American general who was the commander of the Southern Army during the Civil War.

9.

Jim Bowie and Davy Crockett, famous frontiersmen, died in a famous Texas battle against Mexican soldiers. Name this battle.

10.

Name the famous general of World War II who said, "Only those Americans who are willing to die for their country are fit to live."

11.

During the Civil War, Abraham Lincoln quoted the Bible when he said, "A house divided against itself cannot stand." What did he mean?

12.

Name the first American pilot to fly solo across the Atlantic Ocean. What was the name of his plane?

13.

In the 1800s, a famous newspaper publisher, William Randolph Hearst, used his paper to solicit money for a pedestal for a famous statue. Name this statue.

14.

Who was the first signer of the Declaration of Independence? Why did he say he was putting his name in such large writing?

15.

Neil Armstrong, Buzz Aldrin, and 10 other astronauts have done something that no one else has ever done. What is it?

16.

What is the national anthem of our country? Who wrote it?

17.

Who was the American leader in the fight against Mexico in the Texas war for independence?

18.

What American is best known for writing the books *Little Women* and *Little Men?*

19.

In January 1986, a new legal holiday was proclaimed to honor _____.

20.

Who invented the first simple-to-use photograph camera?

Copy these cards onto **pink** card stock.

21.

What famous filmmaker created Mickey Mouse, Donald Duck, and Snow White?

22.

What American changed farming in a big way by inventing the grain reaper in 1831?

23.

Name the cowboy and actor of the 1920s who said, "I never met a man I didn't like."

24.

At Disney World in Florida, one of the main attractions is EPCOT Center. What does EPCOT stand for?

25.

The first mail order company was started in Chicago in 1872 by whom?

26.

On June 4, 1965, the first walk in space was taken by an American astronaut. He later died in a fiery accident in a space vehicle. Name him.

27.

A popular game of today was invented in 1891 by James Naismith because he wanted his physical education students to be able to play indoors during the winter. What game did he invent?

28.

The _____ Award is given each year to the best major league pitcher in baseball. This award is named for the pitcher who first pitched a perfect game in 1904.

29.

Name the American who wrote and published the first American dictionary.

30.

As President, Ronald Reagan named the first woman to the U.S. Supreme Court. Name this woman.

Trim and mount the answer key below on **pink** card stock.

Answer Key for "America, America"

(Pink Deck)

1. Thomas Edison

2. Thomas Jefferson

3. Nathan Hale

4. Dr. Jonas Salk

5. Clara Barton

6. She was the first woman governor in the U.S.

7. Alan Shepard

8. Robert E. Lee

9. Battle of the Alamo

10. General Douglas MacArthur

11. The U.S. would not survive if it remained split on the issue of slavery.

12. Charles Lindbergh; "Spirit of St. Louis"

13. Statue of Liberty

14. John Hancock; so the King of England could read it without his "spectacles."

15. Walked on the surface of the moon

16. "Star Spangled Banner"; Francis Scott Key

17. Sam Houston

18. Louisa May Alcott

19. Martin Luther King, Jr.

20. George Eastman

21. Walt Disney

22. Cyrus McCormick

23. Will Rogers

24. Experimental Prototype Community of Tomorrow

25. Aaron Montgomery Ward

26. Edward H. White

27. Basketball

28. Cy Young

29. Noah Webster

30. Sandra Day O'Connor

The Shot Heard 'Round The World

This game has 70 questions about the American Revolution. Divide the class into groups and give each group 35 questions cards and five "Shot Heard 'Round the World" cards. Give each group its own copy of the rules and the answer key.

Purpose: to practice and review knowledge about the American Revolution

Materials Needed:

- card stock of any color to print game cards and to mount rules and answer key
- laminating materials

Construction:

1. Print game card pages on colored card stock. Laminate pages, then cut the cards apart.
2. Trim the rules box and the answer key boxes. Mount them on the same color of card stock as used for the game cards and laminate them.

 Rules for "The Shot Heard 'Round the World"

This game is for three to four players and one judge.

1. Judge shuffles cards, including those that say, "Shot Heard 'Round the World." Place cards on the table face down.
2. Player to judge's left goes first. Play moves to the left.
3. First player takes a card and reads number and question aloud. Player attempts to answer the question. Judge tells if answer is correct.
4. Players earn points by keeping cards for questions they answered correctly. When a player incorrectly answers a question, the judge reads the correct answer and the card is shuffled back into the card pile to be used again.
5. If you get a card that says "Shot Heard 'Round the World," keep it and take one card from any other player. Then take another turn.
6. Play ends when all cards are gone or when game time is over. Player with the most cards wins. Count "Shot Heard 'Round the World" cards in score.
7. Trade cards with another group to play again.

1.

Give the date and the place where the first shots of the American Revolution were fired.

2.

For about 10 years before 1775, England had been trying to get more control of the colonies. What kind of laws was England passing that upset the colonists?

3.

True or False: The colonies in America sent representatives to the British Parliament to help make the laws for the colonies.

4.

Trouble really began in 1765, when Parliament passed a law that required colonists to buy official stamps to put on legal documents. What was this law called?

5.

The colonies united to protest new tax laws. They formed groups, or committees, to keep in touch. What were these groups called?

6.

In Boston, a group of men formed to take protest actions against England. What was this group of men called?

7.

One form of colonial protest was boycotting. What is a boycott?

8.

The colonies agreed that since they had no representatives in Parliament, England had no right to tax them. The colonies' motto became, "No _____ _____ _____."

9.

In Virginia, a fiery young colonist made a famous speech to protest the Stamp Act. In his speech, he said, "Give me liberty or give me death." Name this Virginian.

10.

Parliament did not realize that the protest to the Stamp Act would be so violent. What did Parliament finally do about the Stamp Act?

11.

In 1767, Parliament passed laws that set taxes on glass, paint, lead, tea and other goods that the colonies imported. What were these laws called?

12.

What is the differences between imported goods and exported goods?

13.

Some colonial merchants avoided paying import taxes by smuggling. What is smuggling?

14.

On March 5, 1770, in Boston, there was a clash between some colonists and British soldiers. Five Americans were killed. This skirmish became known as the _____.

15.

The first American to die in the struggle for independence from England was an African American who died in the Boston Massacre. Who was he?

16.

In December of 1773, to protest a tax on tea, the Sons of Liberty boarded British ships and dumped over 300 chests of tea into the harbor. We know this event as the _____.

17.

To punish Boston for the Boston Tea Party, the English Parliament passed a set of harsh laws known as the _____.

18.

What does intolerable mean?

19.

One of the Intolerable Acts was the Quartering Act. What did the Quartering Act require colonists to do?

20.

To stop the protests against taxes, England sent more soldiers to America. These soldiers had two duties. What were these duties?

21.

How many American colonies were there at the time the Revolution began?

22.

The colonies in America were divided into three groups according to region. Name these three groups.

23.

Name the New England Colonies.

24.

Name the Middle Colonies.

25.

Name the Southern Colonies.

26.

In September, 1774, 12 colonies sent representatives to Philadelphia to discuss the problems with England. What was this meeting called?

27.

Only one colony did not send a representative to the First Continental Congress which met in Philadelphia in September, 1774. What colony was not represented at this meeting?

28.

True or False: All the delegates to the First Continental Congress wanted the American colonies to break away from England and be independent.

29.

What is a delegate?

30.

Most colonists hoped that England and the colonies could reach a compromise. What is a compromise?

31.

Name the general who was the commander of the British troops in Boston when the war started.

32.

Because war seemed near, Massachusetts began to hide stores of arms and ammunition. The most important store of military supplies was in a small town about 20 miles from Boston. Name this town.

33.

In Massachusetts, groups of men were formed to be ready to fight instantly. These groups of men were known as _____.

34.

In 1775, the Prime Minister of England sent General Thomas Gage a message to crush the rebellion in Massachusetts. Name this harsh prime minister.

35.

On April 18, 1775, British soldiers marched to Lexington and Concord to seize colonial supplies and to capture two patriot leaders. Name the two patriots the British wanted.

36.

Two American patriots rode to Lexington and Concord to warn the colonists that "the British are coming." Name these two Americans.

37.

Paul Revere is better known than William Dawes, perhaps because of a famous poem which begins: "Listen, my children, and you shall hear/ Of the midnight ride of Paul Revere." Who wrote this poem?

38.

We remember Paul Revere as a famous American patriot. What trade did Paul Revere follow?

39.

What is a patriot?

40.

Name the American captain who led the colonists as they gathered at Lexington to stop the British soldiers.

41.

At Lexington, the first shot of the American Revolution was fired. Was it an American or a British soldier that fired this first shot?

42.

In the poem, "Concord Hymn," the first shot of the war was called the "shot heard 'round the world." Who wrote this poem?

43.

What did Emerson mean when he called the first shot of the American Revolution the "shot heard 'round the world"?

44.

The first organized battle of the war was fought outside Boston at Breed's Hill, but the battle was named for a different hill nearby. Name this battle.

45.

The Second Continental Congress met and appointed a Virginia plantation owner to be commander-in-chief of the American army. Who was he?

46.

Who wrote these words that encouraged American patriots? "These are the times that try men's souls. The summer soldier...will shrink from the service of (his) country; but he that stands it now, deserves the low and thinks of man and woman."

47.

Shortly after the battle at Lexington, a Vermont patriot took his "Green Mountain Boys" to capture the British Fort Ticonderoga in New York. Name this patriot.

48.

One brilliant American general is remembered because he betrayed his country by agreeing to turn over the American fort at West Point to the British. Name this general.

49.

Name the American patriot who wrote a pamphlet called "Common Sense" in which he said it only made sense for the colonies to separate from England and become independent.

50.

In 1776, the Continental Congress named five men—John Adams, Benjamin Franklin, Robert Livingston, Roger Sherman, and Thomas Jefferson—to do a special job. What was this job?

51.

What document was written to declare American independence from England?

52.

Name the Virginia planter who wrote almost the entire first draft of the Declaration of Independence.

53.

On what date did the Continental Congress approve and adopt the Declaration of Independence?

54.

Who was the first delegate to sign the Declaration of Independence. Why?

55.

Why did John Hancock say that he wrote his name in such large letters when he signed the Declaration of Independence?

56.

Name the building and the city where you can go today to see the original copy of the Declaration of Independence.

57.

About one-third of all Americans did not believe in the fight for independence. They remained true to England. What were these people called?

58.

Name the American who was hanged by the British for spying. His last words were, "I only regret that I have but one life to lose for my country."

59.

True or False: Early in the war, the Americans won many significant battles.

60.

On Christmas Day in 1776, when the American cause seemed about to fail, George Washington's troops scored an important victory by crossing the Delaware River and capturing three regiments of Hessian soldiers at what place?

61.

Who were the Hessians who fought in the American Revolution?

62.

Who was the King of England during the American Revolution?

63.

During the American Revolution, a "first" took place in sea vessels. What kind of sea vessel was developed (by David Bushnell) and first used in the war?

64.

The most famous American naval officer was commander of the Bonhomme Richard. Name this officer who is remembered for his words, "I have not yet begun to fight."

65.

The last major battle of the war took place when the Americans defeated the British at what place in Virginia?

66.

On what date did the war end with the surrender of the British General Cornwallis to George Washington at Yorktown, Virginia?

67.

At the final surrender of the British at Yorktown, Virginia, in 1781, the British band played what song?

68.

The final peace treaty, officially ending the American Revolution, was signed on September 3, 1783. Where was this treaty signed?

69.

Francis Marion, a famous American fighter in South Carolina, led troops in raids against British posts. He gained what famous nickname?

70.

What country of Europe was most helpful to the Americans in winning the war against England?

Shot Heard 'Round the World

Shot Heard 'Round the World

Shot Heard 'Round the World

Shot Heard 'Round the World

Shot Heard 'Round the World

Shot Heard 'Round the World

Shot Heard 'Round the World

Shot Heard 'Round the World

Shot Heard 'Round the World

Shot Heard 'Round the World

Answer Key for "Shot Heard 'Round the World"

1. April 19, 1775; Lexington, Massachusetts

2. Tax laws

3. False

4. Stamp Act

5. Committees of Correspondence

6. Sons of Liberty

7. It is refusing to buy or use a product to get someone to do what you want.

8. ". . . taxation without representation"

9. Patrick Henry

10. It repealed the Stamp Act.

11. Townsend Acts

12. Imports are good brought into the country; exports are sent out

13. It is bringing goods into or out of a country illegally.

14. Boston Massacre

15. Crispus Attucks

16. Boston Tea Party

17. Intolerable Acts

18. Unbearable

19. To keep British soldiers in their homes

20. To keep order and to enforce the new taxes and laws England had passed.

21. Thirteen

22. New England Colonies; Middle Colonies; Southern Colonies

23. Massachusetts; Connecticut; Rhode Island; New Hampshire

24. Pennsylvania; New York; Delaware; New Jersey

25. Virginia; Maryland; Georgia; North Carolina; South Carolina

26. First Continental Congress

27. Georgia

28. False; some saw such action as treason

29. A representative for someone else

30. Each side gives up something in order to reach an agreement

31. General Thomas Gage

32. Concord

33. Minutemen

34. Lord Frederick North

35. John Hancock; Samuel Adams

Answer Key for "Shot Heard 'Round the World" *(cont.)*

36. Paul Revere; William Dawes

37. William Wadsworth Longfellow

38. Silversmith

39. Someone who loves, supports, and defends his country

40. Captain John Parker

41. No one knows who fired the first shot.

42. Ralph Waldo Emerson

43. That shot changed the course of all history

44. Battle of Bunker Hill

45. George Washington

46. Thomas Paine

47. Ethan Allen

48. Benedict Arnold

49. Thomas Paine

50. To write a document to declare the colonies independent from England and to give the reasons why the colonists wanted independence.

51. Declaration of Independence

52. Thomas Jefferson

53. July 4, 1776

54. John Hancock; he was president of the Continental Congress.

55. He wanted King George to be able to read it without his "spectacles".

56. National Archives Building; Washington, D.C.

57. Loyalists or Tories

58. Nathan Hale

59. False

60. Trenton, New Jersey

61. German soldiers who were hired to fight for England.

62. King George III

63. Submarine

64. John Paul Jones

65. Yorktown

66. October 17, 1781

67. "The World Turned Upside Down"

68. Paris, France

69. "Swamp Fox"

70. France

The Blue and the Gray

This Civil War game has 100 questions. Play in small groups or use all the questions with the entire class playing in teams. If several groups play at the same time, make copies of the rules and the answer key for each group.

Purpose: to learn interesting facts about the costliest war in U.S. history

Materials Needed:

- card stock of any color to print game cards and to mount rules and answer key
- laminating materials

Construction:

1. Print the game card pages on colored card stock. Laminate pages, then cut cards apart.
2. Trim the rules box and the answer key boxes. Mount them on the same color of card stock as used for the game cards and laminate them.

Rules for "The Blue and the Gray"

This game is for three to four players and one scorekeeper. Pencil and paper are needed to keep score. Use 30–35 cards for the first round. Lay remaining cards aside.

1. Player to the scorekeeper's left goes first. Play moves to the left.

2. Scorekeeper shuffles cards and spreads cards face down.

3. First player takes a card and reads card number and question aloud. Player attempts to answer the question. Scorekeeper tells if the answer is correct.

4. Scorekeeper keeps score as follows:

   Correct answer: Give the card to the scorekeeper. Scorekeeper records points. Card goes to discard stack. Next player's turn.

   Incorrect answer: Give the card to the scorekeeper. Scorekeeper reads correct answer and then substracts points from player's score. Shuffle cards back into pile to be used again. Next player's turn.

5. When all cards have been used, play another round using a different stack of cards.

6. When game time is over, player with the highest score wins.

1.

How much money did the Civil War cost the U.S. government each day?

A. $1.5 million

B. $2.5 million

C. $3.5 million

(4 points)

2.

Confederate President Jefferson Davis was elected for one term that was half again as long as Lincoln's term in office. How long was Davis' term?

(2 points)

3.

When the South's supply of coal was gone, people formed hard lumps of coal dust, sawdust, sand, and wet clay to burn for heat. What were these lumps called?

(4 points)

4.

One-third of all generals who served in the Civil War graduated from what military academy?

(2 points)

5.

"Confederacy" was the name given to which side, North or South?

(2 points)

6.

The "Union" was the name given to which side, North or South?

(2 points)

7.

Which side, North or South, had more battle deaths during the Civil War?

(3 points)

8.

What famous, brief speech did Lincoln give when he was dedicating a battle cemetery in Pennsylvania?

(2 points)

9.

U.S. President Abraham Lincoln and Confederate President Jefferson Davis were both born in the same state. Name the state.

(3 points)

10.

Name the city and state that was the first capital of the Confederacy.

(3 points)

11.

Montgomery, Alabama, was the capital of the Confederacy from February to May of 1861. After that, the capital was moved to what city in Virginia?

(2 points)

12.

The highest military decoration that is given today was created during the Civil War. What is this decoration called?

(2 points)

13.

How did Rose Greenhow serve the Confederacy during the Civil War?
A. Nurse
B. Spy
C. Cook

(2 points)

14.

Andersonville, in Southern Georgia, was a notorious Confederate _____ during the Civil War.

(2 points)

15.

The first official flag of the Confederacy was called the " _____ ."
A. "Stars and Bars"
B. "Stars and Stripes"
C. "Flag of Dixie"

(3 points)

16.

Julia Ward Howe wrote a famous Civil War song that is still popular today. Name the song.

(2 points)

17.

What small Northern state was the first to issue a call for black troops?

(2 points)

18.

Name the state that was the first to secede from the Union?

(2 points)

19.

A total of how many states seceded from the Union?

(2 points)

20.

The Confederacy extended as far north geographically as the state of _____.

(2 points)

21.

Name two Confederate states that begin with the letter A.

(3 points)

22.

Name two Confederates states that began with the letter T.

(3 points)

23.

Which state was the last to secede from the Union?

(3 points)

24.

Louisa May Alcott, who wrote *Little Women*, served the Union in what way?

A. As a nurse

B. As a spy

C. As a cook

(2 points)

25.

Name the man who became General-in-Chief of the Union Army during the Civil War and was later a U.S. President.

(2 points)

26.

When the war started, Lincoln asked a soldier from Virginia to lead the Union armies. This soldier said no because he wanted to be true to his home state and he later commanded the Confederate armies. Name him.

(2 points)

27.

Where did Confederate president Jefferson Davis spend the first two years after the war ended?

(3 points)

28.

Two new states were admitted to the Union during the Civil War. Name these two states.

(4 points)

29.

Clara Barton, a nurse during the Civil War, later founded a famous organization that still exists today. Name this organization.

(4 points)

30.

Name the place and the city where President Abraham Lincoln was shot by his assassin.

(2 points)

31.

Who assassinated President Abraham Lincoln?

(2 points)

32.

Dorothea Dix served the Union during the Civil War as superintendent of female _____.

(3 points)

33.

Elida Rumsey was admired for her great fund raising efforts for Union soldiers. Because of this, Lincoln asked her in 1862 to have a special ceremony before Congress. She said, "I do." What ceremony was this?

(4 points)

34.

The motto that appears on U.S. coins was first stamped onto coins during the Civil War. What is this motto?

(3 points)

35.

What kind of work did most Union and Confederate soldiers do before the war?

(2 points)

36.

When John Wilkes Booth shot Abraham Lincoln, he was old enough to serve in the House of Representatives, but not old enough to be a Senator or President. He was:
A) 20–25
B) 25–30
C) 30–35

(2 points)

37.

During the war, when food became scarce in the South, egg whites and butter mixed to make a substitute for what beverage additive?

(4 points)

38.

During the Civil War, President Lincoln established a national holiday that Americans quickly "gobbled up" and still enjoy today. Name this holiday.

(2 points)

39.

At Fort Sumter in 1861 Private Daniel Hough became the first Civil War soldier to do what?

(3 points)

40.

Confederate General Stonewall Jackson was often seen sucking on a particular fruit, even during battle. Name this fruit.

(2 points)

41.

Both Abraham Lincoln and Jefferson Davis suffered a family tragedy during the Civil War. What was it?

(4 points)

42.

Who became U.S. President upon the death of Abraham Lincoln?

(2 points)

43.

Name a famous Old West lawman who was a "wild" Union scout during the Civil War.

(3 points)

44.

At the end of the Civil War, the U.S. government offered $100,000 in gold for the capture of what Confederate leader?

(3 points)

45.

What happened at Appomattox Court House in Virginia on April 9, 1865?

(2 points)

46.

During the war, the estate of Robert E. Lee in Arlington, Virginia, was seized by the U.S. government. Today this estate is what national landmark?

(3 points)

47.

General Ambrose E. Burnside had a hairstyle that gave us the name we use to refer to_____.

(2 points)

48.

In 1863, the Union tried to recruit men for the army for three years by making a special offer. What was this offer?

(2 points)

49.

Colonel Paul Joseph Revere died in the Battle of Gettysburg. Who was this Union soldier's famous grandfather?

(2 points)

50.

Union General Winfield Scott was nicknamed because of his love of lavish ceremony. What was his nickname?

(4 points)

51.

During the Civil War, the U.S. army hired Chicago meat packers to provide what troops called "embalmed beef." What was "embalmed beef"?

(4 points)

52.

Union spy Elizabeth Van Lew was called "Crazy Bet." Why?

(3 points)

53.

A Civil War general ran for president against Abraham Lincoln in the 1864 election. Name the general that Lincoln defeated.

(3 points)

54.

When Confederate soldiers were ill, they told the commander they were going to "Company Q." What was "Company Q?"

(4 points)

55.

What famous Confederate General was accidentally killed by a bullet (not a stone) from his own troops at the Battle of Chancellorsville?

(2 points)

56.

This Southern girl was 17 when she first began working as a spy for Gen. Stonewall Jackson in 1862. She was a "belle" who often dressed as a boy to do spying. Name her.

(3 points)

57.

Surrender terms signed at the end of the Civil War allowed Southern troops to keep their _____. Officers were allowed to keep their_____.

(2 points)

58.

Name the important Confederate leader who was blind in his left eye.

(4 points)

59.

To fool Union soldiers, Southern troops used fake cannons cut from logs, painted black and mounted in firing position. What were these fake cannons called?

(4 points)

60.

What biting insects were called "gallinippers" by Confederate troops?

(4 points)

61.

Confederates who faked illness and dropped back to the wagon trains were called "_____" by their fellow soldiers.

(4 points)

62.

Some Union soldiers, after being captured by the South, enlisted in the Confederate army to escape prison life. What were these soldiers called?

(4 points)

63.

The photograph that was made of Lincoln on February 9, 1864, was later used on a monetary bill. On what bill does Lincoln's face appear?

(2 points)

64.

The longest pontoon bridge of the Civil War was 2,200 feet long and used 101 pontoons. What river of Virginia did this bridge span?

(4 points)

65.

Union forces usually named Civil War battles after the nearest _____.

(3 points)

66.

Confederates forces usually named Civil War battles after the nearest _____.

(3 points)

67.

The site of the biggest battle of the Civil War was named for John Gettys, a Pennsylvania settler. Name this battle site.

(2 points)

68.

Black troops first fought in the Civil War at the Battle of Island Mount in 1862, in what so-called border state?

(3 points)

69.

After the Battle of Perryville, water was so scarce that Union army surgeons could not _____ for two days.

(2 points)

70.

Which battle of the Civil War had the largest number of casualties?

(2 points)

71.

When the Union captured this important Southern city, it reopened the Mississippi River for use by the North and it split the South. Name this city.

(2 points)

72.

Two men who would later become the 19th and 25th presidents of the U.S. fought at the Battle of Antietam. Name these two men.

(4 points)

73.

During the war, Confederates attacked as far north as the state that is well known for producing maple syrup. Name this state.

(2 points)

74.

Because of the defeat at Gettysburg, what Confederate general offered to resign?

(2 points)

75.

Where were the first shots of the Civil War fired?

(2 points)

76.

What celebration took place at Fort Sumter, South Carolina, on April 14, 1865?

(3 points)

77.

What sad event took place in Springfield, Illinois, on May 4, 1865?

(2 points)

78.

What document, issued by Lincoln on January 1, 1863, "freed all slaves in areas" in rebellion against the United States?

(2 points)

79.

The following quote describes what Civil War general: "He will take more chances, and take them quicker, than any other general in the country, North or South"?

(3 points)

80.

How was John Wilkes Booth injured as he fled after shooting Abraham Lincoln?

(2 points)

81.

At the battle of Manassas, the great Confederate General Thomas Jackson received a famous nickname when someone said his forces stood like a stone wall. What was the nickname?

(2 points)

82.

Oliver Wendall Holmes was a Captain during the Civil War. What post in government did he hold later in life?

(4 points)

83.

New recruits were being instructed in firing muskets. Their old veteran instructor said, "It's like shooting squirrels, boys, only these squirrels have _____."

(3 points)

84.

What Confederate general said, "It is well that war is so terrible—we should grow too fond of it"?

(3 points)

85.

On Christmas Day, 1863, an escaped slave, Robert Blake, was so heroic in naval battle that he became the first black man in history to get the military's highest award. What award did he get?

(2 points)

86.

The 10th president of the U.S. served in the Confederate Congress and died while the Civil War was in progress. Name this former president.

(3 points)

87.

Before the war, plantations of the South were supported by two main crops. Name them.

(2 points)

88.

Four states (Maryland, Delaware, Kentucky and Missouri) did not leave the Union, but the people were divided in loyalty to North or South. What were these states called?

(2 points)

89.

What does the word "secede" mean?

(2 points)

90.

People who worked to completely do away with slavery were called _____.

(2 points)

91.

Name an escaped slave who became a famous abolitionist and started a newspaper called the *North Star.*

(3 points)

92.

Before the Civil War started, a book titled *Uncle Tom's Cabin* convinced many Northerners that slavery was evil and had to end. Who wrote *Uncle Tom's Cabin?*

(2 points)

93.

When Abraham Lincoln met Harriet Beecher Stowe, author of *Uncle Tom's Cabin*, what did he say to her?

(3 points)

94.

Before the War started, there was a famous secret route to help slaves escape to freedom in the north. What was this escape route called?

(3 points)

95.

The most famous "conductor" on the Underground Railroad was an escaped slave who led over 300 slaves to freedom. Name her.

(2 points)

96.

What is a civil war?

(2 points)

97.

The first major battle of the Civil War was on July 12, 1861. It was fought in northern Virginia along a creek called _____.

(2 points)

98.

Which side—North or South—had better-trained generals?

(2 points)

99.

Which side—North or South—had more soldiers and more supplies?

(2 points)

100.

About 186,000 black men joined the Union army. One of these men, Major Martin Delany, became the first black man in America to achieve what military recognition?

(4 points)

If playing the game with several groups, make a copy of the answer key for each group.

Answer Key for "The Blue and the Gray"

1. B) $2.5 million

2. Six years

3. Fireballs

4. West Point

5. Southern States

6. Northern States

7. North: 110,000; South: 94,000

8. Gettysburg Address

9. Kentucky

10. Montgomery, Alabama

11. Richmond

12. Medal of Honor

13. B) Spy

14. Prison camp

15. A) "Stars and Bars"

16. "Battle Hymn of the Republic"

17. Rhode Island

18. South Carolina

19. Eleven

20. Virginia

21. Alabama; Arkansas

22. Tennessee; Texas

23. Tennessee

24. A) As a nurse in a Union hospital

25. Ulysses S. Grant

26. Robert E. Lee

27. In prison

28. West Virginia; Nevada

29. American Red Cross

30. Ford's Theater in Washington, D.C.

31. John Wilkes Booth

32. Nurses

33. Her wedding

Answer Key for "The Blue and the Gray" *(cont.)*

34. "In God We Trust"

35. Farming

36. B) 25-30

37. Cream for coffee

38. Thanksgiving Day (established on October 20, 1864)

39. First soldier of the Civil War to die in battle

40. Lemon

41. Both had young sons who died.

42. Andrew Johnson

43. "Wild Bill" Hickok

44. Jefferson Davis

45. End of the war; Robert E. Lee surrendered to U.S. Grant

46. Arlington National Cemetery

47. Sideburns

48. Money; $300

49. Paul Revere

50. "Old Fuss and Feathers"

51. Meat in tin cans

52. She pretended to be crazy in order to spy among Southern troops.

53. General George B. McClellan

54. The sick list; quarantine

55. "Stonewall" Jackson

56. Belle Boyd

57. Horses; side arms

58. Jefferson Davis

59. Quaker guns, as the guns would not really fire

60. Mosquitoes

61. "Wagon dogs"

62. "Galvanized Yankees"

63. Five-dollar bill

64. James River

65. Body of water

66. Community

Answer Key for
"The Blue and the Gray" *(cont.)*

67. Gettysburg, Pennsylvania

68. Missouri

69. Wash their hands.

70. Battle of Gettysburg

71. Vicksburg

72. Rutherford B. Hayes and William McKinley

73. Vermont

74. Robert E. Lee; his resignation was not accepted

75. Fort Sumter, South Carolina

76. U.S. flag was raised again—four years to the day after it was forced down.

77. Abraham Lincoln was buried.

78. Emancipation Proclamation

79. Robert E. Lee

80. He broke his leg.

81. "Stonewall" Jackson

82. U.S. Supreme Court Justice

83. Guns

84. Robert E. Lee

85. Medal of Honor

86. John Tyler

87. Cotton and tobacco

88. Border states

89. To formally withdraw from a group or an organization

90. Abolitionists

91. Frederick Douglas

92. Harriet Beecher Stowe

93. "So this is the little woman who started this great war."

94. The Underground Railroad

95. Harriet Tubman

96. A war between people of the same nation

97. Bull Run

98. South

99. North

100. First black man in America to become an Army officer

Make-a-Match Game:
Acronyms and Their Use

Before playing this game, plan a brief study of acronyms and how and why they are used.

Use questions such as the following to lead into the study:

What do you do if an order blank states to include a SASE?

(Send a self-addressed stamped enveloped.)

What does it mean when you read that the "game will start at 4 P.M. EST"?

(The game will start at 4 P.M. Eastern Standard Time.)

What does the boss mean when his memo says "FYI" or "Do this ASAP"?

(The boss means "for your information" and "as soon as possible.")

Why do we use acronyms? (To save writing time and space)

After studying acronyms, play the game to practice and reinforce learning.

Rules for "Make-a-Match Game"

The Make-a-Match Game is made up of five separate games, each played like a concentration or memory game. Each game has different cards. Have groups of three to four students playing simultaneously, then trade cards with other groups to play with different cards.

Note: Each card has a clue to help identify the acronym by putting it within a context.

Purpose: to identify and memorize common acronyms

Materials Needed:

- card stock to print game card pages and to mount rules boxes and answer key boxes in the following colors: blue, yellow, green, orange, and pink
- laminating materials

Construction:

1. Print two copies of each game card page, using the indicated color of card stock. You will have 30 cards of each color. Laminate the pages, then cut cards apart.

2. In order for each group to have its own copy of the rules, make five copies of the rules box. Trim the five boxes. Mount one rules box on each of the five colors of card stock used for the game cards. Laminate them.

3. Each set of cards has its own answer key. Trim each answer key box and mount on the appropriate color of card stock. Laminate them.

Make five copies of the rules. Trim the boxes and mount each on a different color of card stock.

Rules for "Make-a-Match Game"

This game is for three to four players and one judge.

1. Judge shuffles the cards and lays them face down in a 5 x 6 grid.

2. Player to judge's left goes first. Play moves to the left.

3. First player: Turn over two cards to try for a match.

4. If player gets a match, the player must tell what the abbreviation stands for or be able to explain it in order to keep the cards. The judge will tell player if the answer is correct. If the player gives an incorrect answer, the judge should read aloud the correct answer and the card should be placed in a discard pile. Play continues to the left.

5. When all cards are gone or game time is over, each player should count the number of matches he or she has made. The player with the most matches is the winner.

6. If there is time, trade cards with another group and play again.

Make **two** copies of this page on **blue** card stock.

ASAP (Action)	**ABC** (Radio and TV)	**CBS** (Radio and TV)
CPA (Career)	**EDT** (Time)	**GI** (Military)
JAYCEES (Business)	**MST** (Time)	**NASA** (Space)
PDQ (Action)	**PS** (Letters)	**ROTC** (Military)
SASE (Letter)	**SWAT** (Police)	**VEEP** (An official)

Trim and mount this answer key on **blue** card stock.

Answer Key for "Make-a-Match Game"

(Blue Deck)

ASAP—As Soon As Possible (do it quickly)

ABC—American Broadcasting Company

CBS—Columbia Broadcasting System

CPA—Certified Public Accountant (keeps financial records, does taxes, etc.)

EDT—Eastern Daylight Time

GI—Government Issue (usually refers to soldiers)

JAYCEES—Junior Chamber of Commerce (organization of business people; found in many U.S. cities)

MST—Mountain Standard Time

NASA—National Aeronautics and Space Administration (runs U.S. space program)

PDQ—Pretty Darn Quick (Do it now)

PS—Postscript (an addition at the end of a letter)

ROTC—Reserve Officer Training Corps (military group in some high schools and colleges)

SASE—Self—Addressed Stamped Envelope (often needed to be enclosed when ordering something)

SWAT—Special Weapons Action Team (police squad used in especially dangerous situations)

VEEP—Vice President

Make **two** copies of this page on **yellow** card stock.

AD (Calendar)	**AWOL** (Military)	**C/O** (Mailing)
DA (Courts)	**FYI** (On office memos)	**IQ** (Intelligence)
MADD (Drunk Driving)	**NATO** (World Group)	**OPEC** (Organization)
PST (Time)	**RR** (Transportation)	**SOS** (Emergency)
TNT (Dangerous Substance)	**VIP** (An official)	**ZIP** (Mailing)

Trim and mount this answer key on **yellow** card stock.

Answer Key for "Make-a-Match Game"

(Yellow Deck)

AD—"Anno Domini" (Latin for "in the year of our Lord," referring to years since birth of Christ)

AWOL—Absent Without Leave (military expression; refers to one who has left the base without permission)

C/O—In Care Of (mailed to one person "in care of" another person)

DA—District Attorney (government attorney who tries to prove criminals guilty)

FYI—For Your Information

IQ—Intelligence Quotient (a measure of verbal and nonverbal reasoning ability)

MADD—Mothers Against Drunk Driving (organization that works to stop drunk driving)

NATO—North Atlantic Treaty Organization (a group of nations that work together for world defense)

OPEC—Organization of Petroleum Exporting Countries (group of Mideastern countries that export oil)

PST—Pacific Standard Time

RR—Railroad (sign seen at railroad crossings)

SOS—Save Our Ship (originally a call for help at sea, now used as a general call for help)

TNT—Trinitrotoluene (an explosive)

VIP—Very Important Person

ZIP—Zone Improvement Plan (numbers used with mailing addresses to speed delivery)

Make **two** copies of this page on **green** card stock.

AIDS (Medical)	**BLT** (Food)	**CDT** (Time)
DJ (Radio/TV)	**DOT** (Government)	**GIGO** (Computer)
AMA (Organization)	**MIA** (Military)	**NBC** (Radio and TV)
PDT (Time)	**RADAR** (Locating)	**RSVP** (Invitation)
SWAK (Letters)	**TV** (Communication)	**WHO** (Organization)

Trim and mount this answer key on **green** card stock.

Answer Key for "Make-a-Match Game"

(Green Deck)

AIDS—Acquired Immune Deficiency Syndrome (a disease that destroys the body's immune system)

BLT—Bacon, lettuce, and tomato sandwich

CDT—Central Daylight Time

DJ— Disc Jockey (plays music on radio and at dances)

DOT—Department of Transportation (agency of the federal government)

GIGO—Garbage In, Garbage Out (computer term meaning you get from a computer what you put in)

AMA—American Medical Associaton (organization of medical doctors)

MIA—Missing In Action (refers to military persons lost in battle and not known to be dead or alive)

NBC—National Broadcasting Company

PDT—Pacific Daylight Time

RADAR—Radio Detecting and Ranging (used to depict place and speed of moving objects)

RSVP—French for "Respondez s'il vous plait;" translates on an invitation to tell you to let the host or hostess know you will or will not be coming to an event

SWAK—Sealed With A Kiss (put on envelopes to show love)

TV—Television

WHO—World Health Organization (works for improved health around the world)

AM (Time of Day)	**CARE** (Organization)	**CB** (Communication)
CST (Time)	**HUD** (Government)	**IRS** (Government)
MO (Crime)	**NOW** (Organization)	**PBS** (Radio and TV)
POW (Military)	**RAM** (Computer)	**RV** (Transportation)
SCUBA (Underwater)	**TLC** (What everyone needs sometimes)	**UNICEF** (Organization)

Trim and mount this answer key on **orange** card stock.

Answer Key for "Make-a-Match Game"

(Orange Deck)

AM—Ante Meridian (the hours before noon)

CARE—Cooperative for American Relief Everywhere (sends relief packages around the world)

CB—Citizen's Band (radio for talking to others who also have CB radios)

CST—Central Standard Time

HUD—Housing and Urban Development (agency of federal government)

IRS—Internal Revenue Service (collects federal income taxes)

MO—"Modus Operandi" (Latin meaning "method of operation"; used to discuss a criminal's preferred method of committing a crime)

NOW—National Organization of Women (works for women's rights)

PBS—Public Broadcasting System (commercial-free television paid for by private donations)

POW—Prisoner of War

RAM—Random Access Memory (Computer memory that holds information put there by the user)

RV—Recreational Vehicle (large vehicle used for camping)

SCUBA—Self-Contained Underwater Breathing Apparatus (equipment needed for diving)

TLC—Tender Loving Care (affection for someone you love or from someone who loves you)

UNICEF—United Nations International Children's Education Fund (organization that helps impoverished children around the world)

Make **two** copies of this page on **pink** card stock.

AKA (Names)	BC (Calendar)	COD (Payment)
DOE (Government)	EST (Time)	ICBM (Defense)
MDT (Time)	NAACP (Organization)	PA (Communication)
PM (Time)	ROM (Computer)	SADD (Alcohol)
SONAR (Locating)	SPCA (Animals)	UFO (Space)

Trim and mount this answer key on **pink** card stock.

Answer Key for "Make-a-Match Game"

(Pink Deck)

AKA—Also Known As (used when a person uses more than one name; example, Sam Brown a.k.a Greg Hill)

BC—Before Christ (years before the birth of Christ)

COD—Cash On Delivery (mail/packages that must be paid for at the time received)

DOE—Department of Energy (agency of the federal government)

EST—Eastern Standard Time

ICBM—Intercontinental Ballistic Missile (U.S. weapons system)

MDT—Mountain Daylight Time

NAACP—National Association for the Advancement of Colored People (works for equal rights for black Americans)

PA—Public Address (an announcing system)

PM—Post Meridian (afternoon hours)

ROM—Read Only Memory (Computer memory that cannot be changed by the user)

SADD—Students Against Drunk Driving (organization in many high schools; students helping students learn about the dangers of drunk driving)

SONAR—Sound Navigation Ranging (used to detect place and speed of objects underwater)

SPCA—Society for Prevention of Cruelty to Animals (group that works for kind treatment of animals)

UFO—Unidentified Flying Object

Go Exploring!

This 30 card game is a bit of a variation on the old-time game, "Go Fish!" It is a novel way for students to review their knowledge about famous explorers of the New World.

Purpose: match terms with definitions to improve knowledge about the Age of Exploration

Materials Needed:

- card stock of any color to print game cards and to mount rules and answer key
- laminating materials

Construction:

1. Print the game cards on colored card stock. Laminate pages, then cut cards apart.

2. Mount the rules and answer key boxes on card stock of the same color as used for game cards. Laminate them.

Rules for "Go Exploring!"

This game is for three or four players and one scorekeeper. Pencil and paper are needed for keeping score.

1. Scorekeeper shuffles cards and deals seven cards to each player. The remaining deck should be placed face down in a place central to the players. Scorekeeper turns first card up and places it to one side to start a face up discard pile.

2. Player to left of the scorekeeper goes first. Play moves to the left.

3. Begin each turn with player drawing one card from face-down or face-up deck. End each turn by placing one card face up on the discard pile.

4. First player picks up card and makes any possible matches between explorer cards and fact cards.

5. A matching pair is laid face up on table for all to see. Any player may challenge a match. Scorekeeper checks answer key according to card number.

6. If match is incorrect, player picks up cards, takes two additional cards from face-down stack and discards one card to end the turn.

7. If match is correct, player who challenged must take two cards from face down stack. Player with correct match lays the match aside and makes any other possible matches before ending the turn.

8. When one player is out of cards, play stops and points are recorded. Each match is worth 5 points.

9. Shuffle cards and deal to play another round. When game time is over, player with the most points is the winner.

LEIF ERICSON	**1.** The Viking explorer believed to be the first European to reach the New World (in about 1000 A.D.).
BRAZIL	**2.** A South American country that was discovered in 1500 by Portuguese explorer Pedro Alvares Cabral.
NIÑA **PINTA** **SANTA MARIA**	**3.** The 3 ships of Christopher Columbus.
CHRISTOPHER COLUMBUS	**4.** An explorer who "sailed the ocean blue in 1492" for Spain.
CAPE COD	**5.** This sea inlet that borders Massachusetts was named by the English explorer Bartholomew Gosnold who explored the New England coast in 1602.

JAMESTOWN	**6.** The first permanent English colony in the New World.
SIR FRANCIS DRAKE	**7.** This English explorer was the first European to sail around the world.
JOHN CABOT	**8.** This Italian explorer sailed to Nova Scotia and claimed it for England. He also discovered the Grand Banks, one of the world's richest fishing areas.
VENEZUELA	**9.** This South American country was discovered by Alonso de Ojeda, a captain on one of Columbus' ships, who sailed on his own in 1499.
HENRY HUDSON	**10.** An English explorer who has a river in the U.S. and a bay in Canada named for him.

VASCO NUNEZ DE BALBOA	**11.** A Spanish explorer who discovered and named the Pacific Ocean in 1513
NEW ORLEANS	**12.** This U.S. city is home of the Mardi Gras. The city was established in 1718 by a French explorer, Jean Baptiste Le Moyne Bienville.
SAINT AUGUSTINE	**13.** This oldest U.S. city was established by Spanish explorer Pedro de Aviles in 1565.
AMERICAN BUFFALO (BISON)	**14.** This animal is native to the American Great Plains. The first white man to see this animal was the Spanish explorer, Cabeza de Vaca.
HORSE	**15.** This animal was first brought to America by the Spanish explorer Hernando Cortez.

	16.
MEXICO	A North American country that was conquered in 1521 by the Spanish explorer Hernando Cortez.
SAMUEL DE CHAMPLAIN	**17.** This Frenchman explored the St. Lawrence River and founded the great Canadian city of Quebec.
LAKE CHAMPLAIN	**18.** This body of water, named for a French explorer, lies on the boundary between New York and Vermont.
NEW YORK HARBOR	**19.** This body of water was discovered by Giovanni da Verrazano as he explored the Atlantic coast. A bridge there is named for him.
FLORIDA	**20.** This state was discovered and named by Spanish explorer Ponce de Leon as he was searching for the Fountain of Youth.

VINLAND	**21.** In 1960 in Newfoundland, scientists found the remains of this settlement built by Viking explorer Leif Ericson.
VASCO DA GAMA	**22.** The Portuguese explorer who was the first to sail around the southern tip of Africa while searching for a water route to the East.
VIRGINIA	**23.** Visit this state to see the site of the first permanent English colony in the New World.
NIAGARA FALLS	**24.** A popular honeymoon site in the U.S., this great natural wonder was discovered by French explorer Robert de La Salle.
AMERIGO VESPUCCI	**25.** This Italian scrawled his name across a map showing the New World and, guess what?—the newly discovered land was named for him!

LOUIS JOLIET	**26.** This French trapper joined Roman Catholic missionary Father Marquette in exploring the Mississippi River in 1672-1673.
INDIANS	**27.** The name that Christopher Columbus gave to the natives he met when he reached the New World.
HENRY HUDSON	**28.** This explorer traveled for both the English and the Dutch. The New World land that he claimed for Holland became New Netherlands— the first Dutch colony in the New World.
PERU	**29.** This South American country, home of the Incas, was conquered by the Spanish explorer Francisco Pizarro.
NORTH CAROLINA	**30.** Roanoke Island, the site of the "Lost Colony," is located off the coast of this U.S. state.

Answer Key for "Go Exploring!"

1. Leif Ericson

2. Brazil

3. Niña, Pinta, Santa Maria

4. Christopher Columbus

5. Cape Cod

6. Jamestown

7. Sir Francis Drake

8. John Cabot

9. Venezuela

10. Henry Hudson

11. Vasco Nunez de Balboa

12. New Orleans

13. Saint Augustine

14. American buffalo (bison)

15. Horse

16. Mexico

17. Samuel de Champlain

18. Lake Champlain

19. New York Harbor

20. Florida

21. Vinland

22. Vasco da Gama

23. Virginia

24. Niagara Falls

25. Amerigo Vespucci

26. Louis Joliet

27. Indians

28. Henry Hudson

29. Peru

30. North Carolina

Using a Dictionary of Quotations

A dictionary of quotations such as Bartlett's is unfamiliar to many students, who may not realize how useful such a resource can be for making correct attributions of a speech or as springboards for their own writing. Before playing the next two games, "Who Said That?" and "Match-a-Quote," plan one or two lessons to teach students about dictionaries of quotations.

Give students opportunity to use such dictionaries by asking them to research people from history who have said the familiar and perhaps not-so-familiar things on which the games are based. For this purpose, there is a research worksheet to go with each game. Give each student copies of the worksheets. Assign one or more quotes to each student. Ask students to conduct the following research:

- Use a dictionary of quotations to find the source of the quote.

- Use an encyclopedia and other resources to find out interesting or even funny facts about the author of the quote.

- Find out the circumstances that led to what was said, e.g., was it part of a speech or said during the heat of battle?

- Find out when and where the quoted material took place.

- Were there other people present at the time? Who? Did any of them have a quotable response? What was it?

- What does the quote mean? Why you think the author of the quote felt the need to say it?

- Can the quote be applied to our lives today? Why or why not?

Ask each student to share the information they found. As the speaker of each quote is named in class, the students can write these names on their worksheets, which they should then study. After students have completed their study of quotations, play the games. Both games are played with cards being dealt to players who then try to make matches. You may wish to allow students to use their research worksheets when they first play the game.

Play Variation:

Divide the class into two teams. Give out the cards having the names of the speakers. A card reader (teacher or student) reads the quote aloud and a player from either team who knows the answer stands up. If the answer is correct, that player's teams gets a point. If the answer is incorrect, the opposing team receives a point. If no student can answer, the card reader gives the name of the speaker and the quotation. The person holding the quotation card turns it in and the opposing team receives a point.

More than one quote may be included from the same speaker. In this case, the first speaker to stand and give the correct answer gets the point.

Who Said That?
Worksheet

Write the name of the person who made each of the following statements.

1. "Early to bed and early to rise makes a man healthy, wealthy and wise."

_____

2. "History does not long entrust the care of freedom to the weak or the timid."

_____

3. "The inventor is a man who looks around upon the world and is not content with things as they are."

_____

4. "Leisure is the time for doing something useful."

_____

5. "I only regret that I have but one life to lose for my country."

_____

6. "We have met the enemy and he is us."

_____

7. "I had rather be right than be President."

_____

8. "If we do not want to die together in war, we must make a plan to live together in peace."

_____

9. "When written in Chinese, the word 'crisis' is composed of two characters— one represents danger and the other represents opportunity."

_____

10. "First in war, first in peace, first in the hearts of his countrymen."

_____

11. "A government big enough to give you all you want is big enough to take it all away."

_____

12. "I know not what course others may take; but as for me, give me liberty or give me death."

_____

13. "Where liberty dwells, there is my country."

_____

14. "There never was a good war or a bad peace."

_____

15. "That's one small step for man; one giant leap for mankind."

_____

16. "All men are created equal, ...they are endowed by their Creator with certain unalienable rights,...among these are Life, Liberty and the Pursuit of Happiness."

_____

Who Said That?
Worksheet *(cont.)*

17. "There is no substitute for hard work."

18. "No race can prosper till it learns that there is as much dignity in tilling a field as in writing a poem."

19. "Ask not what your country can do for you, ask what you can do for your country." (*Note:* The first person to say these words was not John F. Kennedy.)

20. "The only thing we have to fear is fear itself."

21. "Taxation without representation is tyranny."

22. "We cannot learn from one another until we stop shouting at one another."

23. "You can fool all the people some of the time, and some of the people all the time, but you cannot fool all the people all of the time."

24. "It is well that war is so terrible, or we should grow too fond of it."

25. "You must obey this, . . . he that will not work shall not eat."

26. "To be prepared for war is one of the most effectual means of preserving peace."

27. "Genius is two percent inspiration and 98% perspiration."

28. "I have noticed that nothing I never said ever did me any harm."

29. "Be always sure you are right—then go ahead."

30. "I never did anything worth doing by accident, nor did any of my inventions come by accident; they came by work."

Answer Key for "Who Said That?" Worksheet

1. Benjamin Franklin
2. Dwight D. Eisenhower
3. Alexander Graham Bell
4. Benjamin Franklin
5. Nathan Hale
6. Pogo, character created by Walter Kelly
7. Henry Clay
8. Harry S. Truman
9. John F. Kennedy
10. Henry Lee describing George Washington
11. Barry Goldwater
12. Patrick Henry
13. Benjamin Franklin
14. Benjamin Franklin
15. Neil Armstrong
16. Thomas Jefferson
17. Thomas Edison
18. Booker T. Washington
19. John F. Kennedy; Warren G. Harding said it first
20. Franklin D. Roosevelt
21. James Otis
22. Richard M. Nixon
23. Abraham Lincoln
24. Robert E. Lee
25. Captain John Smith
26. George Washington
27. Thomas Edison
28. Calvin Coolidge
29. Davy Crockett
30. Thomas Edison

Match-a-Quote
Worksheet

Write the name of the person who made each of the following statements.

1. "Some books are to be tested, others to be swallowed, and some few to be chewed and digested."

   _____

2. "It is better that ten guilty persons escape than one innocent suffer."

   _____

3. "Liberty, too, must be limited in order to be possessed."

   _____

4. "Little drops of water, little grains of sand, make the mighty ocean and the pleasant land. So the little minutes, humble though they be, make the mighty ages of eternity."

   _____

5. "Tell me what company thou keepest, and I'll tell thee what thou art."

   _____

6. "In war, whichever side may call itself the victor, there are no winners, but all are losers."

   _____

7. "Be wiser than other people if you can, but do not tell them so."

   _____

8. "Whatever is worth doing at all is worth doing well."

   _____

9. "Never in the field of human conflict was so much owed by so many to so few."

   _____

10. "When you have nothing to say, say nothing."

    _____

11. "Imitation is the sincerest form of flattery."

    _____

12. "To be conscious that you are ignorant is a great step to knowledge."

    _____

13. "No man is an island, entire of itself, every man is a piece of the Continent, a part of the main."

    _____

14. "The louder he talked of his honor, the faster we counted our spoons."

    _____

15. "The only reward of virtue is virtue; the only way to have a friend is to be one."

    _____

16. "The reward of a thing well done is to have done it."

    _____

17. "Nothing can bring you peace but yourself."

_____

18. "Life is mostly froth and bubble/Two things stand like stone/Kindness in another's trouble/Courage in your own."

_____

19. "No young man believes he shall ever die."

_____

20. "I am the master of my fate; I am the captain of my soul."

_____

21. "Life is made up of sobs, sniffles, and smiles, with sniffles predominating."

_____

22. "If at first you don't succeed, try, try again."

_____

23. "Will you walk into my parlour? said a spider to a fly; it's the prettiest little parlour that ever you did spy."

_____

24. "Beauty is altogether in the eye of the beholder."

_____

25. "I think that I shall never see/A poem lovely as a tree . . . poems are made by fools like me. But only God can make a tree."

_____

26. "Two men look out through the same bars; one sees the mud, and one the stars."

_____

27. "No man is good enough to govern another man without that other's consent."

_____

28. "We cannot be free men if this is to be a land of slavery. Those who deny freedom to others, deserve it not for themselves."

_____

29. "The man who makes no mistakes does not usually make anything."

_____

30. "Look out how you use proud words. When you let proud words go, it is not easy to call them back."

_____

Answer Key for "Match-a-Quote" Worksheet

1. Francis Bacon
2. Sir William Blackstone
3. Edmund Burke
4. Julia Carney
5. Miguel De Cervantes
6. Neville Chamberlain
7. Phillip Chesterfield
8. Phillip Chesterfield
9. Winston Churchill
10. Charles Colton
11. Charles Colton
12. Benjamin Disraeli
13. John Donne
14. Ralph Waldo Emerson
15. Ralph Waldo Emerson

16. Ralph Waldo Emerson
17. Ralph Waldo Emerson
18. Adam Gordon
19. William Hazlitt
20. William Henley
21. O. Henry (William Sydney Porter)
22. William Erickson
23. Mary Howitt
24. Margaret Hungerford
25. Joyce Kilmer
26. Frederick Langbridge
27. Abraham Lincoln
28. Abraham Lincoln
29. Edward John Phelps
30. Carl Sandburg

Who Said That?

After completing the worksheets on page 232-233, students can practice and reinforce their knowledge of quotations by playing this game.

Purpose: to learn famous historical quotations

Materials Needed:

- card stock of any color to print game cards and to mount rules and answer key
- laminating materials

Construction:

1. Print the game cards onto colored card stock. Laminate the pages, then cut the cards apart.
2. Trim the rules and answer key boxes. Mount on card stock of the same color as used for game cards. Laminate them.

Rules for "Who Said That?"

This game is for three players and one scorekeeper. Pencil and paper are needed for keeping score.

1. Player to the left of scorekeeper goes first. Play moves to the left.
2. Scorekeeper shuffles cards and deals seven cards to each player. The remaining deck should be placed face down in a place central to players. Scorekeeper turns first card up and places it to one side to start the discard pile.
3. Begin each turn with player drawing one card from face down or face up deck. End each turn by placing one card face up on discard pile.
4. First player picks up face up or face down card. Player makes any possible matches between quotation cards and author cards. A matching pair is laid face up on table for all to see. Any player may challenge a match. Scorekeeper checks answer by card number.
5. If match is incorrect, player picks up cards, takes two additional cards from face down deck, and discards one card to end turn.
6. If match is correct, player who challenged must take two cards from face-down deck. Player with correct match lays the match aside and makes any other possible matches before ending the turn.
7. When one player is out of cards, play stops and points are recorded. Each match is worth five points.
8. Shuffle cards and deal to play another round. At end of playing time, player with the most points is the winner.

1.

"Early to bed and early to rise makes a man healthy, wealthy, and wise."

2.

"History does not long entrust the care of freedom to the weak or the timid."

3.

"The inventor is a man who looks around upon the world and is not contented with things as they are.

4.

"Leisure is the time for doing something useful."

5.

"I only regret that I have but one life to lose for my country."

6.

"We have met the enemy and he is us."

7.

"I had rather be right than be president."

8.

"If we do not want to die together in war, we must make a plan to live together in peace."

9.

"When written in Chinese, the word "crisis" is composed of two characters—one represents danger and the other represents opportunity."

10.

"First in war, first in peace, first in the hearts of his countrymen."

11.

"I know not what course others may take; but as for me, give me liberty or give me death."

12.

"Where liberty dwells, there is my country."

13.

"There never was a good war or a bad peace."

14.

"That's one small step for man; one giant leap for mankind."

15.

"...all men are created equal,. . . they are endowed by their Creator with certain unalienable rights,. . . among these are Life, Liberty and the Pursuit of Happiness."

16.

"There is no substitute for hard work."

17.

"No race can prosper till it learns that there is as much dignity in tilling a field as in writing a poem."

18.

"If we do not want to die together in war, we must make a plan to live together in peace."

19.

"Ask not what your country can do for you, ask what you can do for your country."

20.

"The only thing we have to fear is fear itself."

21.

"Taxation without representation is tyranny."

22.

"We cannot learn from one another until we stop shouting at one another."

23.

"You can fool all the people some of the time, and some of the people all the time, but you cannot fool all the people all of the time."

24.

"It is well that war is so terrible, or we should grow too fond of it."

25.

"You must obey this,...he that will not work shall not eat."

26.

"To be prepared for war is one of the most effectual means of preserving peace."

27.

"Genius is two percent inspiration and 98 percent perspiration."

28.

"I have noticed that nothing I never said ever did me any harm."

29.

"Be always sure you are right—then go ahead."

30.

"I never did anything worth doing by accident, nor did any of my inventions come by accident; they came by work."

Benjamin Franklin	**Dwight D. Eisenhower**
Alexander Graham Bell	**Benjamin Franklin**
Nathan Hale	**Walt Kelly**
Henry Clay	**Harry S. Truman**
John F. Kennedy	**Henry Lee**

Patrick Henry	Benjamin Franklin
Benjamin Franklin	Neil Armstrong
Thomas Jefferson	Thomas Edison
Booker T. Washington	Harry S. Truman
John F. Kennedy	Franklin D. Roosevelt

James Otis

Richard M. Nixon

Abraham Lincoln

Robert E. Lee

Captain John Smith

George Washington

Thomas Edison

Calvin Coolidge

Davy Crockett

Thomas Edison

Answer Key for "Who Said That?" Game

1. Benjamin Franklin
2. Dwight D. Eisenhower
3. Alexander Graham Bell
4. Benjamin Franklin
5. Nathan Hale
6. Walt Kelly
7. Henry Clay
8. Harry S. Truman
9. John F. Kennedy
10. Henry Lee
11. Patrick Henry
12. Benjamin Franklin
13. Benjamin Franklin
14. Neil Armstrong
15. Thomas Jefferson
16. Thomas Edison
17. Booker T. Washington
18. Harry S. Truman
19. John F. Kennedy; Warren G. Harding
20. Franklin D. Roosevelt
21. James Otis
22. Richard M. Nixon
23. Abraham Lincoln
24. Robert E. Lee
25. Captain John Smith
26. George Washington
27. Thomas Edison
28. Calvin Coolidge
29. Davy Crockett
30. Thomas Edison

Match-a-Quote

This game, like "Who Said That?", should be preceded by asking students to research quotes and complete the accompanying worksheet on page 235-236. Print this game on different color than used for "Who Said That?" in order to avoid confusion.

Materials Needed:

- card stock (Use a different color than for "Who Said That?")
  to print game cards and to mount rules and answer key
- laminating materials

Construction:

1. Print the game cards on colored card stock. Laminate pages, then cut cards apart.
2. Trim the rules and answer key boxes. Mount on card stock of same color as used for game cards. Laminate them.

Rules for "Match-a-Quote"

This game is for three players and one judge. Pencil and paper are needed for keeping score.

1. Player to the left of judge goes first. Play moves to the left.

2. Judge shuffles cards and deals seven cards to each player. The remaining deck should be placed face down in a place central to players. Judge turns first card up and places it to one side to start the discard pile.

3. Begin each turn with player drawing one card from deck or discard pile. End each turn by placing one card face up on discard pile.

4. First player picks up face up or face down card. Player makes any possible matches between quotation cards and author cards. A matching pair is laid face up on table for all to see. Any player may challenge a match. Judge checks answer by card number.

5. If match is incorrect, player picks up cards, takes two additional cards from face down deck, and discards one card to end turn.

6. If match is correct, player who challenged must take two cards from face-down deck. Player with correct match lays the match aside and makes any other possible matches before ending the turn.

7. When one player is out of cards, play stops and points are recorded. Each match is worth five points.

9. Shuffle cards and deal to play another round. At end of playing time, player with the most points is the winner.

1.

"Some books are to be tasted, others to be swallowed, and some few to be chewed and digested."

2.

"It is better that ten guilty persons escape than one innocent suffer."

3.

"Liberty, too, must be limited in order to be possessed."

4.

"Little drops of water, little grains of sand, Make the mighty ocean and the pleasant land. So the little minutes, humble though they be, Make the mighty ages of eternity."

5.

"Tell me what company thou keepest, and I'll tell thee what thou art."

6.

"In war, whichever side may call itself the victor, there are not winners, but all are losers."

7.

"Be wiser than other people if you can, but do not tell them so."

8.

"Whatever is worth doing at all is worth doing well."

9.

"Never in the field of human conflict was so much owed by so many to so few."

10.

"When you have nothing to say, say nothing."

11.

"Imitation is the sincerest form of flattery."

12.

"To be conscious that you are ignorant is a great step to knowledge."

13.

"No man is an island, entire of itself; every man is a piece of the Continent, a part of the main."

14.

"The louder he talked of his honor, the faster we counted our spoons."

15.

"The only reward of virtue is virtue; the only way to have a friend is to be one."

16.

"The reward of a thing well done is to have done it."

17.

"Nothing can bring you peace but yourself."

18.

"Life is mostly froth and bubble/Two things stand like stone/Kindness in another's trouble/Courage in your own."

19.

"No young man believes he shall ever die."

20.

"I am the master of my fate: I am the captain of my soul."

21.

"Life is made up snobs, sniffles, and smiles—with sniffles predominating."

22.

"If at first you don't succeed, try, try again."

23.

"Will you walk into my parlour?
Said a spider to a fly;
'It's the prettiest little parlour
That ever you did spy."

24.

"Beauty is altogether in the eye of the beholder."

25.

"I think that I shall never see
A poem lovely as a tree...
Poems are made by fools like me,
But only God can make a tree."

26.

"Two men look out through the same bars: one sees the mud, and one the stars."

27.

"No man is good enough to govern another man without that other's consent."

28.

"We cannot be free men if this is...to be a land of slavery. Those who deny freedom to others, deserve it not for themselves."

29.

"The man who makes no mistakes does not usually make anything."

30.

"Look out how you use proud words. When you let proud words go, it is not easy to call them back."

Francis Bacon

Sir William Blackstone

Edmund Burke

Julia Carney

Miguel De Cervantes

Neville Chamberlain

Phillip Chesterfield

Phillip Chesterfield

Winston Churchill

Charles Colton

Charles Colton	Benjamin Disraeli
John Donne	Ralph Waldo Emerson
Ralph Waldo Emerson	Ralph Waldo Emerson
Ralph Waldo Emerson	Adam Gordon
William Hazlitt	William Henley

O. Henry (William Sydney Porter)

William Hickson

Mary Howitt

Margaret Hungerford

Joyce Kilmer

Frederick Langbridge

Abraham Lincoln

Abraham Lincoln

Edward John Phelps

Carl Sandburg

Answer Key for "Match-a-Quote"

1. Francis Bacon
2. Sir William Blackstone
3. Edmund Burke
4. Julia Carney
5. Miguel De Cervantes
6. Neville Chamberlain
7. Phillip Chesterfield
8. Phillip Chesterfield
9. Winston Churchill
10. Charles Colton
11. Charles Colton
12. Benjamin Disraeli
13. John Donne
14. Ralph Waldo Emerson
15. Ralph Waldo Emerson
16. Ralph Waldo Emerson
17. Ralph Waldo Emerson
18. Adam Gordon
19. William Hazlitt
20. William Henley
21. O. Henry (William Sydney Porter)
22. William Hickson
23. Mary Howitt
24. Margaret Hungerford
25. Joyce Kilmer
26. Frederick Langbridge
27. Abraham Lincoln
28. Abraham Lincoln
29. Edward John Phelps
30. Carl Sandburg

Three Branches, One Government

This game can be played by groups of two to three students or be used by individual students for practice and review.

Purpose: to review the work of the executive, legislative, and judicial branches of the Federal government

Materials Needed:

- card stock in two different colors to print game cards to mount rules and answer key
- laminating materials

Construction:

1. Print the five category headings (page 255) on card stock in one color. Laminate the page, then cut the cards apart.
2. Print the game cards pages on a card stock of a second color. Laminate pages, then cut the cards apart.
3. Trim rules and answer key boxes. Mount on the same color as game cards. Laminate them.

Rules for "Three Branches, One Government"

This game is for two to three players and one judge.

1. Players sit in a semi-circle so that all may see the cards.
2. Judge lays out the five category headings in this order:

   President

   Supreme Court

   House Of Representatives

   Senate

   Both House And Senate

3. Judge shuffles remaining cards and places them face down.
4. Player sitting to the left by the "President" heading goes first. Play continues to the left.
5. First player: Take a card. Read card number and statement aloud. Tell the body of government into which the card fits. Place the card under the proper category heading.
6. Judge says whether or not the answer is correct and scores as follows:

   Correct answer: Win 2 points.

   Incorrect answer: Lose 2 points. Card is removed and goes to bottom of stack.

7. When all cards are used, player with the most points is the winner.

Copy these category heading cards on a different color stock than the game cards on the pages that follow.

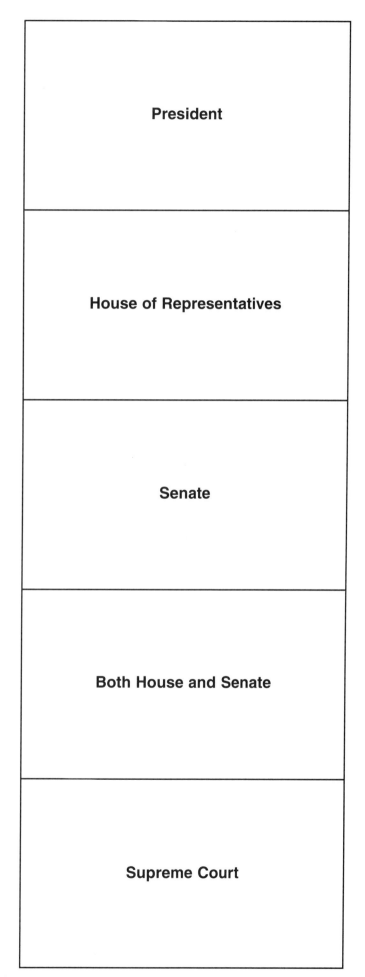

President

House of Representatives

Senate

Both House and Senate

Supreme Court

1.

Congress

2.

Chosen by the Electoral College

3.

Elected by the people

4.

Appointed by the president

5.

Decides what the laws say and if laws agree with the U.S. Constitution

6.

Commander-in-Chief of all U.S. military forces

7.

Makes laws for the entire county

8.

Can sign bills so they can become laws

9.

Can veto a bill to keep it from becoming a law

10.

Can override the president's veto by $^2/_3$ vote

11.	12.
Heads the Executive Branch	Legislative Branch
13.	**14.**
Judicial Branch	Has nine justices
15.	**16.**
William Rehnquist	Head member is called the Speaker of the House
17.	**18.**
Head member is the vice president of the U.S.	Head member is the chief justice
19.	**20.**
Meets in the U.S. Capitol Building	Has the final word on all U.S. laws

21.

Members serve in office for life unless they resign or are removed from office

22.

Must be re-elected every two years

23.

Must be re-elected every six years

24.

Must be re-elected every four years

25.

Can serve unlimited terms if re-elected

26.

Can serve only two terms

27.

Makes sure the laws are carried out or enforced

28.

Has two members from each state

29.

Has members based on each state's population

30.

Must be at least 35 years old to hold this office

31.

Must be at least 30 years old to hold this office

32.

Must be at least 25 years old to hold this office

33.

Can vote to impeach the U.S. president

34.

Holds the trial that determines if the president should be removed from office

35.

Has a president pro tempore to preside when the leader cannot be there

36.

Must be a native-born American citizen to hold this office

37.

Can declare war

38.

Appoints a "cabinet" to help run the country

39.

Has 435 members

40.

Has 100 members

Answer Key for "Three Branches, One Government"

1. Both House and Senate
2. President
3. Both House and Senate
4. Supreme Court
5. Supreme Court
6. President
7. Both House and Senate
8. President
9. President
10. Both House and Senate
11. President
12. Both House and Senate
13. Supreme Court
14. Supreme Court
15. Supreme Court
16. House of Representatives
17. Senate
18. Supreme Court
19. Both House and Senate
20. Supreme Court
21. Supreme Court
22. House of Representatives
23. Senate
24. President
25. Both House and Senate
26. President
27. President
28. Senate
29. House of Representatives
30. President
31. Senate
32. House of Representatives
33. House of Representatives
34. Senate
35. Senate
36. President
37. Both House and Senate
38. President
39. House of Representatives
40. Senate

The Law of the Land

This game has 120 questions, plus 10 "We the People" cards and 10 "Law Breaker" cards. To play, divide the class into four groups, shuffle the question cards, and give each group an equal number of game cards, "We the People" cards, and "Law Breaker" cards. Make a copy of the rules and answer key for each group. Groups can play a round and then trade cards with another group to play again.

Purpose: to practice and review knowledge about the U.S. Constitution

Materials Needed:

- card stock of any color to print game card pages and to mount rules and answer key
- laminating materials

Construction:

1. Print game card pages on colored card stock. Laminate pages, then cut cards apart.
2. Make four copies of rules and answer key so that each group has a copy of each.
3. Trim rules and answer key boxes. Mount them on the same color card stock as used for the game cards. Laminate them.

Rules for "The Law of the Land"

This game is for four groups, each with three or four players, and one judge.

1. Judge shuffles all cards and spreads them face down.

2. Player to judge's left goes first. Play moves to the left.

3. First player takes a card and reads card number and question aloud. Player attempts to answer the question. Judge tells if answer is correct.

4. Players earn points by keeping cards for questions they have answered correctly. When a player incorrectly answers a question, the card is shuffled back into the card pile to be used again.

5. If you get a card that says "We the People," keep that card, take one card from any other player, and take another turn.

6. If you get a card that says "Law Breaker," give that card and one of the cards in your hand to the player on your right. Your turn is over.

7. When all cards are used or when game time is over, players count cards. The player with the most cards is the winner.

1.

What was the first plan of government that the Continental Congress drew up to unite the colonies?

2.

The Articles of Confederation failed because it did not provide for a strong enough _____.

3.

In what year and in what city was the present Constitution written?

4.

Name the building in which the delegates met and wrote the Constitution.

5.

How many of the 13 states were represented at the Constitutional Convention?

6.

Name the state or states that did not have delegates at the Constitutional Convention.

7.

Give the month, date, and year when the Constitution was signed by the delegates to the Constitutional Convention.

8.

Name the man who was chosen as the president of the Constitutional Convention.

9.

One delegate at the Constitutional Convention took very extensive notes. It is because of his notes that we know what went on at the Convention. Who was this man?

10.

After the Constitution was written, a copy was sent to each state for its vote. How many states had to approve the Constitution before it could go into effect?

11.

Some states said they would approve the Constitution only if amendments were added to give some basic rights to individuals. Ten amendments were added. These first ten amendments are called _____.

12.

Name the state that was first to sign the new Constitution.

13.

Three states voted unanimously to accept the new Constitution. What does the word unanimous mean?

14.

After nine states ratified the new Constitution it went into effect. What does ratify mean?

15.

After nine states approved the new Constitution it went into effect. In what year did this happen?

16.

The Constitution has an introduction that is called the _____.

17.

How many articles does the U.S. Constitution have?

18.

How many amendments have been added to the Constitution since it was first written?

19.

What part of the Constitution summarizes the reasons why the Constitution was written?

20.

How many branches does the federal government have?

21.

Name the branches of the federal government.

22.

Which branch of the federal government is responsible for making the laws for the country?

23.

Which branch of the federal government is responsible for carrying out the laws passed by Congress?

24.

Which branch of the federal government is responsible for interpreting the laws passed by Congress?

25.

What official is the head of the Executive Branch?

26.

Which article of the Constitution tells who can be a president of the U.S. and what a president can and cannot do?

27.

Which article of the Constitution tells how Congress is set up and what powers Congress does and does not have?

28.

How many members are there in Congress?

29.

Name the two houses of Congress.

30.

How many members are there in the Senate?

31.

How many members are there in the House of Representatives?

32.

How is it determined how many members each state may have in the House of Representatives?

33.

How is it determined how many members each state may have in the Senate?

34.

Each member of the House of Representatives is elected for a term of _____ years.

35.

Each member of the Senate is elected for a term of _____ years.

36.

What title is given to the leader of the House of Representatives?

37.

What official serves as the president of the Senate?

38.

Who is currently serving as the Speaker of the House?

39.

Who is currently serving as president of the Senate?

40.

What title is given to the person who presides over the Senate when the vice president cannot be there?

41.

What is the minimum age requirement for a person being elected to the House of Representatives?

42.

What is the minimum age requirement for a person being elected to the Senate?

43.

To be elected president of the United States, a person must be how old?

44.

True or False: To be president of the United States, a person must be a native-born citizen.

45.

Which house of Congress has the power to impeach a U.S. president?

46.

If a U.S. president is impeached, which house of Congress holds the trial?

47.

Which U.S. official presides over a trial of impeachment of a U.S. president?

48.

What does impeach mean?

49.

In order to find an impeached president guilty, what percentage of senators present must vote guilty?

50.

All senators are not elected at the same time. One-third of the Senate is elected every _____ years.

51.

Things that happen in Congress each day are written down in the _____.

52.

What government agency has the power to issue currency or money?

53.

What government agency has the power to declare war?

54.

True or False: The senators who represent your state are elected by all the voters in the state.

55.

Name the two senators who represent your state in Congress.

56.

True or False: The person who represents you in the House of Representatives is elected by all the voters in your state.

57.

What is a Congressional district?

58.

Name the person who represents your district in the House of Representatives.

59.

Who elects the president of the United States?

60.

How many members are in the Electoral College?

61.

What is it called when a president refuses to sign into a law a bill that Congress has passed?

62.

A president may ignore a bill from Congress for 10 days and let it become law without his signature. What is it called when a president does this?

63.

Congress may vote a bill into law even if the president has vetoed it. What percent of each house must vote for the bill to override the veto?

64.

How long is one term for a U.S. president?

65.

How many members does each state have in the Electoral College?

66.

How many terms may a U.S. president be elected for?

67.

Currently, a president may only serve for two terms. One previous president in U.S. history was elected to four terms. Name this President?

68.

Congress may not pass an ex post facto law. What is an *ex post facto* law?

69.

What is the longest that a U.S. president can possibly serve? Explain.

70.

What is the name of the day on which a newly elected president officially takes office?

71.

On what month and date is Inauguration Day?

72.

If a president dies or cannot serve due to illness, who takes over the office of president?

73.

If a vice president takes over as president and then dies before he can appoint a new vice president, who would become president?

74.

What government official appoints judges to the Supreme Court?

75.

Who must approve appointments to office that are made by the president?

76.

What government agency is the "highest court in the land?"

77.

What is the president's group of chief advisors called?

78.

What title is given to the official that heads the Department of State, the Department of Education, and other executive departments?

79.

Which group in the federal government has the power to admit new states into the union?

80.

The Supreme Court is headed by what official?

81.

Who is the chief justice of the Supreme Court?

82.

How many associate judges are on the Supreme Court?

83.

In 1967, the first African American man was appointed to serve on the Supreme Court. Name him.

84.

In 1981, the first woman was appointed to serve on the Supreme Court. Name her.

85.

What body of the government has the power to propose amendments to the Constitution?

86.

What fraction of Congress must vote for a proposed amendment to the Constitution before it can be sent to the states for vote?

87.

What fraction of the states must approve a new amendment before it can be added to the Constitution?

88.

For how long is a Supreme Court justice appointed?

89.

What amendment says that a person has the right not to testify against himself?

90.

The 19th amendment says that no person may be denied the right to _____ because of his or her gender.

91.

What government official has the power to make treaties with other nations?

92.

The Constitution says that the president must give an annual address before Congress. What is the address called?

93.

The only crime defined in the Constitution is treason. What is treason?

94.

Article III of the Constitution says that any person who is accused of a crime has the right to what kind of trial?

95.

What group in the federal government has the power to decide the punishment for treason?

96.

Each branch of the federal government has the power to control the power of the other two branches. This is called the system of _____.

97.

Article IV says that a person who commits a crime and then flees to another state must be returned to the state where the crime was committed. What is this called?

98.

Article V of the Constitution explains how the Constitution can be _____.

99.

Which amendment of the Constitution provides for freedom of speech?

100.

The Fourth Amendment of the Constitution says that a person's house may not be searched unless the authorities have a _____.

101.

The Fifth Amendment says that before a person can be tried, he must be indicted. What is an indictment?

102.

The Fifth Amendment says that no person can be subjected to double jeopardy. What does this mean?

103.

The Fifth Amendment says that a person cannot be punished for a crime without due process of law. What is due process of law?

104.

The Sixth Amendment says that if a person cannot afford an attorney, one will be appointed for him or her. Who appoints this attorney?

105.

The Eighth Amendment says that excessive bail cannot be required of any accused person. What is bail?

106.

The 12th Amendment says that if the Electoral College is unable to reach a majority vote for a president, then the president is chosen by the _____.

107.

The 13th Amendment says that _____ shall not be allowed in the United States.

108.

The 15th Amendment says that no person can be denied the right to _____ because of his or her race.

109.

The 16th Amendment gives Congress the power to collect _____.

110.

The only amendment ever repealed was the 18th Amendment. What did this amendment prohibit?

111.

Only one amendment has ever been repealed. What does repeal mean?

112.

The 12th Amendment places limits on the number of _____ one president may have.

113.

The 26th Amendment gives the right to vote to what group of people?

114.

A crime that is very serious and punishable by a long jail sentence or large fine is a _____.

115.

A less serious crime that is punishable by short jail sentence or small fine is called a _____

116.

A legal document issued to an inventor to protect his or her invention from being copied is called a _____.

117.

Those who write articles, stories, books or songs are not issued patents. Their legal protection is called a _____.

118.

What is the legal term for going broke?

119.

What fraction of Congress must vote "yes" before a member can be expelled from office?

120.

A court order requiring that a person being held in jail must be shown good reasons why he is being held is called a writ of _____ _____.

We the People

We the People

We the People

We the People

We the People

We the People

We the People

We the People

We the People

We the People

Law Breaker

Law Breaker

Law Breaker

Law Breaker

Law Breaker

Law Breaker

Law Breaker

Law Breaker

Law Breaker

Law Breaker

Answer Key for "The Law of the Land"

1. Articles of Confederation
2. Central government
3. 1787 in Philadelphia, Pennsylvania
4. Independence Hall
5. Twelve
6. Rhode Island
7. September 17, 1787
8. George Washington
9. James Madison
10. Nine
11. The Bill of Rights
12. Delaware
13. Everyone votes the same way
14. To approve or to agree to
15. 1788
16. Preamble
17. Seven
18. Twenty-seven
19. Preamble
20. Three
21. Executive branch; legislative branch; judicial branch

22. Legislative branch
23. Executive branch
24. Judicial branch
25. President of the United States
26. Article II
27. Article I
28. 535
29. Senate; House of Representatives
30. 100
31. 435
32. It is based on the population of the state.
33. Each state has two senators.
34. Two
35. Six
36. Speaker of the House
37. Vice President of the United States
38. Will vary
39. Will vary
40. President pro tempore (usually called the "pro tem")

Answer Key for
"The Law of the Land" *(cont.)*

41. Twenty-five years old

42. Thirty years old

43. Thirty-five years old

44. True

45. House of Representatives

46. Senate

47. Chief Justice of the U.S. Supreme Court

48. To accuse of crimes while in office

49. Two-thirds of the Senators present

50. Two

51. Congressional Record

52. Congress

53. Congress

54. True

55. Answers will vary.*

56. False

57. An area of population that sends an elected representative to Washington, D.C.

58. Answers will vary.*

59. Electoral College

60. 538 (Equal to members in Congress plus 3 for Washington, D.C.)

61. Veto

62. Pocket veto

63. Two-thirds of each house

64. Four years

65. Same as total of senators and representatives in Congress

66. Two

67. Franklin D. Roosevelt

68. A law that would punish a person for something that was not against the law when it was done.

69. Two years of an unexpired term of another president, plus two elected terms for a total of ten years

70. Inauguration Day

71. January 20

72. Vice President

73. Speaker of the House

74. President of the United States

75. Senate

76. Supreme Court

77. Cabinet

78. Secretary

79. Congress

80. Chief Justice

*Answers 55 and 58 are left blank to be filled in with answers appropriate for your state.

Answer Key for
"The Law of the Land" *(cont.)*

81. Answers will vary

82. Eight

83. Thurgood Marshall

84. Sandra Day O'Connor

85. Congress

86. Two-thirds of each house

87. Three-fourths

88. For life

89. Fifth Amendment

90. Vote

91. President

92. State of the Union Address

93. Giving aid or information to the enemy

94. A trial by jury

95. Congress

96. Checks and balances

97. Extradition

98. Amended

99. First Amendment

100. Search warrant

101. A formal charge that accuses a person of a crime

102. No person may be tried a second time for the same crime if he has been tried once and found not guilty.

103. Following correct procedures according to the laws

104. The court

105. Money an accused person can pay as guarantee not to run away while awaiting trial

106. House of Representatives

107. Slavery

108. Vote

109. Income taxes

110. The buying and selling of alcoholic beverages

111. To remove or do away with

112. Terms

113. Eighteen-year-olds

114. Felony

115. Misdemeanor

116. Patent

117. Copyright

118. Bankruptcy

119. Two-thirds

120. Habeas corpus

Economics Vocabulary

This game has thirty economics terms that players must match with definitions.

Purpose: match terms with definitions to improve knowledge of economics vocabulary

Materials Needed:

- card stock of any color to print game cards and to mount rules and answer key
- laminating materials

Construction:

1. Print the game cards on colored card stock. Laminate the pages, then cut cards apart.

2. Trim the rules box and the answer key box. Mount on card stock of the same color as used for the game cards. Laminate them.

Rules for "Economics Vocabulary"

This game is for three or four players and one judge. Pencil and paper are needed for keeping score.

1. Judge shuffles cards and deals seven cards to each player. Stack remaining cards face down. Turn first card face up and place to one side to start discard pile.

2. Player to left of the dealer goes first. Play moves to the left.

3. Begin each turn by drawing one card from either the face down or face up deck. Player makes any possible matches between vocabulary word cards and definition cards.

4. A matching pair is laid face up on table for all to see. Any player may challenge a match. Judge checks answer key according to card number.

5. If match is incorrect, player must return incorrect match to cards in hand, take two additional cards from face down deck, and discard one card to end turn.

6. If match is correct, any player who challenged the match must take two cards from the face down deck. Player with correct match lays that match aside and makes any other possible matches before ending his or her turn.

7. When one player is out of cards, play stops. Points are recorded. Each match is worth five points.

8. Shuffle and deal to play another round. When game time is over, player with most points is the winner.

1. Items such as land, buildings, tools, money, etc., that are used in the production of other goods $	**CAPITAL RESOURCES** $
2. Someone who uses goods or services $	**CONSUMER** $
3. The study of the manufacture, distribution, sale, and use of goods and services $	**ECONOMICS** $
4. How much in the way of goods and services people want and are able and willing to buy at a given price $	**DEMAND** $
5. Materials that are produced for people to buy or things that can be seen and touched $	**GOODS** $

6. Jobs that people do for other people in return for pay $	**SERVICES** $
7. Things in nature for which man has found use $	**NATURAL RESOURCES** $
8. The amount of money that a company makes after all the costs of running the business have been paid $	**PROFIT** $
9. The amount of money that must be spent to get a certain good or services $	**COST** $
10. A person who makes goods or provides services $	**PRODUCER** $

11. The amount of a product that is available for people to purchase $	**SUPPLY** $
12. Things that people would like to have but can live without, such as TVs $	**WANTS** $
13. Things that people must have in order to survive, such as food $	**NEEDS** $
14. The things you give up when making a choice between two things $	**OPPORTUNITY COST** $
15. Making and providing goods and services for people to buy $	**PRODUCTION** $

16.	
People with skills who do a job $	**HUMAN RESOURCES** $
17.	
Money paid to someone in exchange for the use of that person's property $	**RENT** $
18.	
Money that is paid to a worker for the amount of time that has been worked $	**WAGES OR SALARY** $
19.	
When there are not enough goods and services to satisfy the wants and needs of the people $	**SCARCITY** $
20.	
A business owner $	**ENTREPRENEUR** $

 #2313 Social Studies Games

21. The person who hires someone else to do work $	**EMPLOYER** $
22. A person who is hired by someone else to do a job $	**EMPLOYEE** $
23. When people do the jobs that they are interested in and do best $	**SPECIALIZATION** $
24. Money that is paid on a loan by the borrower for the use of that money $	**INTEREST** $
25. A general rise in the price level of goods and services $	**INFLATION** $

26. Times when people are out of work and business are doing badly $	**RECESSION** $
27. Shares of a business that can be bought and sold $	**STOCK** $
28. Someone who puts money into a business hoping to make a profit $	**INVESTOR** $
29. A contest between businesses or people to get the most customers or the best price $	**COMPETITION** $
30. Different jobs needed in production are divided among various workers $	**DIVISION OF LABOR** $

Answer Key for "Economics Vocabulary"

1. Capital resources
2. Consumer
3. Economics
4. Demand
5. Goods
6. Services
7. Natural Resources
8. Profit
9. Cost
10. Producer
11. Supply
12. Wants
13. Needs
14. Opportunity Cost
15. Production

16. Human Resources
17. Rent
18. Wages or Salary
19. Scarcity
20. Entrepreneur
21. Employer
22. Employee
23. Specialization
24. Interest
25. Inflation
26. Recession
27. Stock
28. Investor
29. Competition
30. Division of Labor

Copy this page to create more game cards of the appropriate size.

Resources and Web Sites

Resources

Arnold, Nick. *Voyages of Exploration*. Thomson Learning, New York, 1995.

Ayer, Eleanor. *Our Great Rivers and Waterways*. Millbrook Press, 1994.

Boatner, Mark M., III. *Encyclopedia of the American Revolution*. David McKay Company, 1974.

Carruth, Gorton. *The Encyclopedia of American Facts and Dates*. HarperCollins, 1993.

Fritz, Jean. *Around the World in 100 Years*. G. P. Putnam, 1994.

Grant, Neil. *History Eye Witness—Explorers*. Silver Burdett, 1982.

Hyman, Robin. *NTC's Dictionary of Quotations*. National Textbook Company, 1994.

Irizarry, Carmen. *Passport to Mexico*. Franklin Watts, 1987.

Jacobson, Karen L. *Egypt (A New True Book)*. Children's Press, 1990.

James, Ian. *Inside Japan*. Franklin Watts, 1987.

Partin, Ronald L. *The Social Studies Teacher's Book of Lists*. Prentice Hall, 1992.

Rubel, David. *Encyclopedia of the Presidents and Their Times*. Scholastic, 1994.

Schaum, John Walter. *Fifty Songs—Fifty States*. Schaum Publishers, 1971.

Stienecker, David L. *Discovering Geography—Countries*. Marshall Cavendish Corp., 1998.

Tames, Richard. *Passport to Japan*. Franklin Watts, 1988.

Wright, David and Jill. *Illustrated World Atlas*. Warwick Press, 1987.

Zeman, Anne and Kelly, Kate. *Everything You Need to Know about Geography Homework* (*A Desk Reference for Students and Parents*). Scholastic, 1997.

Web Sites

http://www.execpc.com/~dboals/boals.html

History/Social Studies Web Site for K–12 Teachers: History sources; a decision-making game; creative projects, resources for parents, and much more.

http://www.eduplace.com/ss/index.html

Houghton Mifflin Social Studies Center: Current events; over 25 outline maps; discussion forum to chat about social studies with educators all over the world; GeoNet Game—a fun geography game based on the national geography standards.

http://sunsite.unc.edu/cisco/cisco-home.html

Cisco Educational Archives and Resources Catalog (CEARCH): From the University of North Carolina. Help for educators and schools in finding educational resources on the Web.

http://www.iglou.com/xchange/ece/index.html

eMail Classroom Exchange: Students can meet and correspond with other students from around the world. Over 5,400 classrooms participating. Great for cultural, history, science, and geography projects.

http://www.westnet.com/~rickd/Teachers.html

Eastchester Middle School: Web resources helpful to Middle School Teachers. Access current events, American history (great Civil War stuff!), flags of the U.S. and the world (current and historic), the White House, Congress, U.S. government, world history, and the *Titanic*.

http://grid.let.rug.nl/ahc/hist.html

WWW Services for Historians: Information about countries on all seven continents.

http://www.cwc.lsu.edu/civlink.html

Index of Civil War Information available on the Internet: Over 2,100 links to information, fun and factual, about the Civil War.

http://www.historychannel.com/historychannel/thisday/

This Day in History: Enter any day and find significant happenings that occurred on that day in history.

http://www.ukans.edu/history/

Index of Resources for Historians: From the University of Kansas. Twenty-five hundred connections to historical information arranged alphabetically by subject and name.

http://www.ucr.edu/h-gig/horuslinks.html

Horus' Web Links to History Resources: From the University of California, Riverside Department of History. Information and conversation on historical issues.